from: BRET

Hi, Anybody!

Why I Love Baseball and What I'd Do to Fix It

By Denny Matthews with Matt Fulks

Foreword by David Glass

Hi, Anybody!

Why I Love Baseball and What I'd Do to Fix It

By Denny Matthews with Matt Fulks

Foreword by David Glass

Presented by

www.ascendbooks.com

10 9 8 7 6 5 4 3 2 1

Printed in the United States of America

ISBN-13: 978-0-9817166-6-4

ISBN-10: 09817166-6-0

Library of Congress Cataloging-in-Publications Data available upon request

Editor: Lee Stuart

Cover & book design: The Covington Group, Kansas City, Missouri

Front cover photos courtesy of Chris Vleisides

www.ascendbooks.com

DEDICATIONS

This book is dedicated to all of the Royals fans who make it such a joy to broadcast games every night and who make books like this — about the game we all love — possible.

Presenting Sponsors:

Chapter Sponsors:

TABLE OF CONTENTS

ACKNOWLEDGMENTS

A lot of people helped to bring this book to fruition. We'll go ahead and say now that if we forget to mention you by name, still know that we were thinking about you. For whatever that's worth!

To Laurie Bollig, Lee Stuart, Bob Snodgrass and the rest of the gang at Ascend Books for your patience, guidance and willingness to get this book on the shelves. You guys helped take what was going to be an updated book and turned it into a completely new project.

To John Sprugel at Metro Sports for your assistance and guidance.

To Dave and Kathy Minich for giving Matt a hideaway in the middle of Missouri so he could work on this project.

To the Kansas City Royals organization, particularly the media relations staff of Mike Swanson, Dave Holtzman, Colby Curry and Dina Wathan, for your research assistance as well as support and encouragement during this project. You guys are some of the best in the business.

To the club's public relations staff, especially Lora Grosshans and Toby Cook, for helping scout some photo shoots, even during stadium construction in the hectic week before the season opener, and for your ideas.

To Neil Harwell for your support and friendship to both authors.

To Herk Robinson and Dave Witty for your guidance and for sharing some terrific stories.

To each of the former Royals players and executives — approximately 35 in all — whose previous interviews with Denny or Matt helped form many of the stories here.

To two people who have brought the Royals alive through photos and art, Chris Vleisides and John Martin.

Thanks, also, to Chris Browne and Rich Brown for your stories.

To David Glass for your willingness to write a great Foreword. Kansas City is lucky to have you as the owner of the Royals.

We each would like to thank our parents, brothers and extended families for their encouragement throughout our lives. Finally, Matt would like to thank his wife, Libby, and children — Helen, Charlie and Aaron — for your support and putting up with the insanity that is deadline.

Thank you, all.

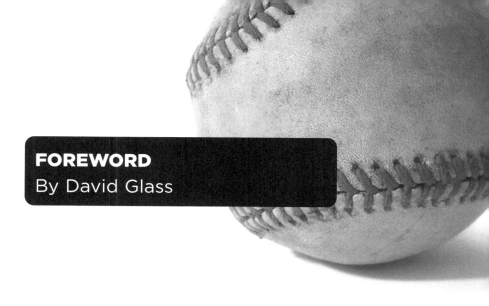

Baseball is the greatest game in the world. At least it is to me. My love affair with the sport — as is true for so many people — began as a child.

I grew up in a small southern Missouri town, Mountain View, where there wasn't much to do in the summers except play baseball. All of the kids played baseball, seemingly, all day, every day when the weather was nice. I think all of us wanted to play for the St. Louis Cardinals, which, at that time, was the only team west of the Mississippi.

I was obsessed with baseball. My life's ambition was to become a Major League Baseball player. The only thing that kept me from realizing my dream, unfortunately, is that I didn't have the talent to play. But I never lost the desire.

One day in 1946, a gentleman who lived in Mountain View loaded up a bunch of us boys and took us to Sportsman's Park in St. Louis to see an afternoon game. My first Major League game! Wow...I was hooked right off the bat. It was so fascinating to see that Major League diamond with the smooth infield and wonderful green grass. I'd never seen anything like it, especially considering the rocky infield and patchy grass, at best, that we were used to playing on. When you're a child, that is heady stuff. I'll never forget that experience. My love for the game of baseball and the St. Louis Cardinals was magnified later that year when St. Louis won the World Series. Nothing inspires interest like success.

The next year, 1947, I went back to Sportsman's Park to see the Cardinals play the Brooklyn Dodgers, which was a big rivalry in those days. That's when I saw Jackie Robinson for the first time. He blew me away with his skill, especially on the base paths. I hated seeing him on first base because he took the longest lead I'd ever seen; it seemed like he was halfway to second base. He'd taunt the pitcher, just daring him to throw over there. As with my first game, that's a game that I'll always remember.

Those memories are so vivid for me largely because in those days in towns across the country similar to Mountain View, Missouri, we experienced baseball primarily on the radio. Everybody in our town listened to the Cardinals' games on the radio with broadcasters Harry Caray and Gabby Street. Griesedieck Brothers Beer sponsored the broadcasts. Harry Caray used to sign on: "This is Harry Caray and the old sergeant Gabby Street..." Gabby Street was the manager of the Cardinals in the 1930s after his playing career as a catcher. He was the color commentator, even though he was a grouchy old guy. Of course, Harry kept it going. Even back then, he had his signature home run call: "It might be...it could be...it is!" You get hooked on that stuff as a kid. That certainly was the case for me.

In many ways today, more than 60 years later, even with all of the technological advancements and gadgets we have, baseball remains a wonderful sport on the radio. The Kansas City Royals have been lucky to have some outstanding announcers, but the one thread between the fans and the team since the club's first season in 1969 has been Denny Matthews.

Denny's work and love of the game has helped instill a passion for baseball in fans — young and old — for more than 40 years.

The first time Denny and I met, we realized that we shared similar baseball backgrounds. Both of us became baseball junkies in the beginning with a real love for the game. He also grew up as a Cardinals fan. He's from the Bloomington, Illinois, area, which is an interesting place because it's about halfway between Chicago and St. Louis. Half of the people were probably Cubs fans and the other half were Cardinals fans. Fortunately, because of his father's love of the Cardinals, Denny chose the right team.

Denny grew up wanting to be like Don Blasingame, a second baseman for the Cardinals in the 1950s. I was a second baseman, also, so I always thought Don Blasingame was a neat player. Interestingly, Don married Walker Cooper's daughter, who was Miss Missouri one year. (Cooper was one of Blasingame's teammates with the Cardinals in the 1950s. Of course, that was at the end of Cooper's career and early in Blasingame's.)

In *Hi, Anybody!*, you'll read about Denny's love for the Cardinals, as well as his well-deserved acknowledgment from the Baseball Hall of Fame in 2007.

Another thing you'll read about is Denny's realignment plan. From time to time, Denny, who is one of the most detailed people I've ever met, comes over to where I'm sitting during a game and visits. He always brings his scorecard with him and meticulously keeps score. He's not superficial as far as baseball is concerned; he has a strong desire to see the game flourish. So, during one of our visits, we started talking about ways to improve the game and make it more competitive and interesting for the fans. At the time in the mid-1990s, realignment was a hot topic.

As Denny and I were discussing realignment possibilities, he offered to come up with a plan that I could present to Major League Baseball. His plan, as you'll read, is based on a team's geography. In essence, it would drastically change the current American League and National League, but it would develop natural rivalries that we won't experience currently. Some people call Denny's plan "regional realignment," others call it "radical realignment." Either way, it was a plan that I liked then and I still like today.

Keep in mind, baseball is a game of tradition. Not a lot has changed during the past 100 years. Sure, the athletes are a little different, a little better perhaps, but the game's pretty much the same. Some of that is by design, but a lot of it on the Major League level is because of the tradition. You wouldn't believe how many people, particularly the old timers, say, "We do it that way because we've always done it that way," when hearing a new idea.

The idea of breaking the league down into three divisions and creating the wild card is radical, particularly for the traditionalists. People oftentimes forget that when many of us started watching Major League Baseball, there were eight teams in each league. There wasn't a playoff system, so teams had to win their league to go to the World Series. You win, you're in; you lose, you're out.

I shared Denny's plan with Commissioner Bud Selig and other owners. Unfortunately, it was met with some resistance, which I understand. Tradition. With Interleague play and wild-card playoffs, I think many of those traditionalists have come around and now realize that some change is good.

Even though I pushed Denny's plan for awhile, not everyone saw the benefits of it for the game. Denny devised it and I was carrying the ball with it. Unfortunately, I didn't get my part done, because, retrospectively, had we realigned along those geographic lines, I feel baseball would be better today for it.

Still, in spite of all of us, the game prospers and survives today. There have been lots of poor decisions made in baseball as I look back over the years, but the game is so strong that it keeps going. Regardless of what football people want to say, baseball remains America's pastime.

As far as the future of the Royals, I really feel the club is headed in the right direction. Frankly, once you get to .500, 10 games one way or the other can decide if you make the playoffs. Ten games above .500 make you very competitive. Then you have a shot to be in the mix each year. I think we're on the edge of that right now.

I look forward to Denny Matthews remaining an integral part of the excitement for fans while the Royals continue this surge. As a baseball fan myself, I've always enjoyed listening to Denny on the air. He has knowledge of the ins and outs of the game. He describes the action very well, while telling us why that play happened the way it did.

If you just take the years that Denny has been a broadcaster, he truly is the voice of the Royals. But he's also a voice for baseball. He has experienced things that most of us, who are not as close to the game, have not experienced. He has seen both the highest of the highs and the lowest of the lows.

This new book, *Hi, Anybody!*, gets into Denny's philosophies on the game and lessons he's taken from it. With the things he's experienced, he's uniquely qualified, I think, to write a book such as this. I hope you enjoy getting to know more about a man who we're fortunate to have as a member of the Kansas City Royals family.

— *David Glass*

I think the Royals are headed in the right direction under the leadership of Dan Glass (left) and David Glass.

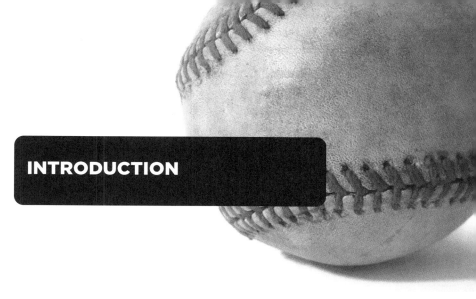

INTRODUCTION

Have you ever started a project at work or home, thinking it's going to be quick and relatively simple, only to get into it and it becomes a monster you weren't expecting? In the end, though, the project usually turns out much better than the one you anticipated finishing quickly.

That's a perfect description of this book. Since the summer of 2007, Denny and I have been throwing around the idea of updating our *Tales from the Royals Dugout* book. After all, Kauffman Stadium was going to be getting a facelift and the team was undergoing a facelift with a new General Manager, Dayton Moore. Oh, yeah, and there was this honor thing that Denny won called the Ford C. Frick Award from the Baseball Hall of Fame.

For whatever reason, we kept putting it off and putting it off. That is, until January 2009, at the Royals FanFest. Denny and I were signing copies of that previous book, and we kept hearing: "When are you guys going to write another book with a chapter on the Hall of Fame?"

So, we began throwing the idea around for the next several days, and decided to talk with publisher Bob Snodgrass about it. Bob was an integral part of the previous two books Denny and I wrote together, *Tales from the Royals Dugout* and *Play by Play*, which we co-wrote with our good friend and Denny's long-time broadcasting partner, Fred White.

Bob liked the idea but his only request was that, instead of simply updating the previous book, we try to come up with at least 60 percent new material. With the guidance of Bob and editor Lee Stuart, the result is a book that is largely new material.

You're going to find a few of Denny's favorite stories in this book. There are certain anecdotes from his career and certain characters he's come across that are worth mentioning several times over.

On the flip side, if you're looking for a book about the history of the Royals, this isn't the one for you. In fact, by design, we don't get into a lot of specific games. *Hi, Anybody!* is more about the people Denny has met and the things he has learned during his career, which began with the Royals in the club's first season, 1969.

Hi, Anybody! gets into some of Denny's philosophies while offering a behind-the-scenes look at the game of baseball. Along the way, you'll be treated to some poignant and humorous "inside" stories from many of the men who have made the Royals franchise one of the best in baseball. You'll also get to read Denny's responses to several questions from fans. These are set off in special boxes at the conclusion of every chapter.

There's even a story behind the title of this book. You've probably heard Denny and countless other announcers open a broadcast with a phrase such as "Hi, everybody," or "Good evening, everybody," or "Welcome, everybody." Something along those lines.

When Denny first started with the Royals in 1969, the original "voice" of the Royals was legendary announcer Buddy Blattner. Sometimes, when the Royals were about to start a game in front of a small crowd, especially late in the season, or were playing on the west coast with games starting in the Kansas City area at 9:35 p.m. — or any other game that might not have a large audience— right before going on the air Bud would call out, "Hi, anybody!"

Appropriately, while we were trying to come up with the perfect title for this book, Denny remembered Buddy's phrase late one night. It seemed to convey the theme of this book perfectly.

As Denny told me while we were writing this, "The neat thing is, almost everybody in this country has played baseball in some form or another — baseball, softball, stickball, Wiffle ball. Almost everybody can identify with baseball and things we're talking about, which are the inner-workings of an athlete or a person."

We hope you find *Hi, Anybody!* as interesting and fun to read as it was to write.

— *Matt Fulks, April 2009*

CHAPTER ONE
"I'm Calling to Make Your Day"

I never got into broadcasting for any type of accolade. Shoot, do any of us get into any profession or start any job with that in mind? Of course not, especially when you're starting with a new organization at a young age.

For me, that meant starting just a few years out of college at Illinois Wesleyan, working with the expansion Royals in 1969. It was a dream job for an announcer in his mid-20s. And, it was a job that I felt would return me, eventually, closer to my roots in central Illinois, with either one of the Chicago teams or the St. Louis Cardinals. Little did I know then that I'd enjoy Kansas City so much and become so comfortable working with the Royals, that I'd reach a point in my career when people would start mentioning my name with the Baseball Hall of Fame.

Sure enough, someone pointed out to me in 1998, when I was pondering my future, that if I were to broadcast in 2000, that I would have broadcast exclusively for the same team, without interruption, in five different decades. Wow! Fewer than 10 guys in the history of the game had done that. Each of those guys was in the broadcaster's wing of the National Baseball Hall of Fame. Admittedly, the idea of that accolade, the Ford C. Frick Award, crept into the back of my mind. It was flattering to hear that, but it wasn't necessarily an impetus for me to continue with the Royals.

A few years later, in 2005, from what I understand, I finished in the top three for the award. The next year, I've been told that Gene Elston beat me by one vote.

So, I started thinking that 2007 could be my year. The exact date I'd find out was Thursday, February 22. The morning went along without any phone calls. Once the clock passed 10:30 — 11:30 at the Hall of Fame — I figured it wasn't meant to be. At least not this time.

Disappointed, I went about my normal day-to-day activities. It was nice enough outside that I was going to survey some of the trees and shrubs outside, pay bills, return phone calls, and so on.

At 11:15, I put the stamp on my final bill for the day. The phone rang.

"Hello?"

"Denny, this is Dale Petroskey with the Hall of Fame. I'm calling to make your day."

Boy, did he ever! He went on to tell me how I was going to receive the award in Cooperstown on July 29 along with long-time *St. Louis Post-Dispatch* writer Rick Hummel, the J.G. Taylor Spink Award winner, and former players Cal Ripken Jr. and Tony Gwynn.

Talk about a class of stability. Hummel spent his entire career with the same newspaper, Ripken spent his entire career with the Baltimore Orioles, Gwynn spent his whole career with the San Diego Padres, and then I spent my career with the Royals.

Frankly, after speaking to Dale Petroskey, I had a tingle all over. I didn't want to get my hopes too high that week, but the butterflies started flying

> "As I've often written, I think Denny's been underestimated nationally, and taken for granted too often by fans and critics who should know better. ... Believe it or not, some guys politic or hire publicists, but Denny has not schmoozed for the Hall of Fame. He's not engaged in self-promotion. He's not engaged in jock shock or screaming or publicizing himself. He has let his work speak for itself, which I admire enormously."
>
> — Curt Smith, author and historian, who was a member in 2007 of the 20-member electorate that chooses the Frick winner

on Wednesday. Even though you know you're a finalist for the award and you hear you've been extremely close before, actually winning isn't something you can count on. As Frank White has said numerous times, when it comes to a human vote with emotion, anything is possible. It was a tremendous honor to be on the list of candidates, but it sure was nice to be off that list.

That phone call started a flurry — a barrage, really — of phone calls from various well wishers, ranging from Royals owner David Glass to Hall of Fame announcers Ernie Harwell and Milo Hamilton. (The Hall of Fame hadn't even made the "official" announcement yet!)

Once the word got out, my phone didn't stop ringing. I exchanged calls with family members, my Royals partner of 25 years, Fred White, called, as did other friends and numerous media outlets. My co-author, Matt Fulks, has joked about how he came over to the house, and we talked for maybe 15 minutes during his 2-hour stay. It was crazy, but I wanted to soak as much of it in as possible.

Up to that point, I'd never experienced anything like that. Besides the chaos, there was the surreal thought of my name and photo in the broadcaster's wing of the Baseball Hall of Fame in Cooperstown, alongside the likes of Harwell and Hamilton and Vin Scully and Jack Brickhouse and Joe Garagiola.

"Denny's a special guy. He has passion for this organization, which is obvious in his broadcasts. He's seen so many games and so many personalities, and he's been able to relay that to the fans over the air, which is not an easy thing to do. Especially during the 1970s and '80s, when not as many games were on TV, everyone relied on Denny's voice to tell them what was happening on the field and whether a guy should've gotten to a ball or how it was hit, or whatever. For how long he's been here, it's obvious that he's relayed a pretty good message, which is a tremendous credit to him."

— Joe Randa, who played for the Royals, 1995-96 and then 1999-2004

One of my earliest baseball memories is being in the house with the St. Louis Cardinal games on the radio with Garagiola, Harry Caray and Jack Buck broadcasting. My dad, George "Matty" Matthews, was a big

Stan Musial was my dad's favorite player.

Cardinals fan, especially of Stan Musial, so my love of the Redbirds soon followed suit.

My favorite player was St. Louis second baseman Don Blasingame, who batted left-handed. I, likewise, was a left-handed hitting second baseman, so I guess that's why I started following him so closely. After careful consideration, I sent a letter to Blasingame one day, requesting an autograph. I had never done that before and haven't done it since. He returned a signed black-and-white postcard picture of himself that I have to this day.

As the summer sounds of those three men came out of our radio — although, mainly just Caray and Buck, since Garagiola wasn't part of that team for very long — I would lie on the floor with my baseball cards of the two teams playing placed in front of me. I pulled out the lineups of each team, and then changed the top card whenever a new batter came to the plate, while Buck and Caray painted wonderful word descriptions of what was happening on the field.

Besides listening to Cardinal games, we could also pick up Chicago Cubs games on radio. The Cubs had a broadcaster then by the name of Jack Quinlan who was very good. He died in a car accident during spring training in Arizona in the 1960s. Brickhouse, who was instrumental in helping me get the job with the Royals, was doing Cubs games on TV, but we were out of their viewing area. The only TV game we got was the Saturday Game of the Week.

So, to take a long look at the list of previous Ford C. Frick Award winners, even today, is humbling because it gives you that feeling that you grew up with these guys. A lot of them affected my style and the way I've gone about things. Even many of those who didn't directly influence my career were very supportive and encouraging when I started in the business.

Having gone through induction into the Royals Hall of Fame in 2004, I had an idea — albeit on a different scale — of what to expect in terms of the emotions and preparing my speech. But I didn't know exactly how incredible those days in July would be.

Denny's Hall of Fame Diary

Since several people who have gone through Hall of Fame weekend told me what type of a whirlwind it would be, my co-author Matt Fulks and I thought it would be cool to document each day's events with some type of journal. Matt was going to be in Cooperstown that weekend both as a friend to me and as a writer for KCMetroSports.com, the website for Kansas City's sports TV station, Metro Sports.

"I was probably as happy about Denny being honored by the Hall of Fame as he and his family were. It was an acknowledgment that was well deserved. He had an enormous amount of support for a long time from a number of the better-known announcers. The late Jack Buck worked hard to get Denny recognized, as did Joe Garagiola and others of that same magnitude who knew Denny and appreciated how good he is."

— David Glass, Royals owner

So we talked each night during Hall of Fame weekend for what turned out to be a daily "Denny's Diary" for Metro Sports. The following is taken from those three diary entries.

That's fellow Ford C. Frick Award winner Bob Uecker and me long before either of us ever thought we'd get the call from the Hall of Fame.

Friday, July 27

Leading up to this weekend, George Brett had passed along words of encouragement and some advice from his Hall of Fame experience in 1999. One thing he told me was to do my best to slow down when possible and let everything soak in a little. I see what he meant.

Busy.

That's the best way to describe my first 36 hours or so here in Cooperstown. Our flight left the Kansas City area Thursday morning and headed to Bloomington, Ill., to pick up my mom, my brother Mike, his son Kyle, and one of my other nephews, Scott. We flew to the airport in Utica, N.Y., where a representative of the Hall of Fame waited to pick us up and drive us to Cooperstown. The rest of the afternoon was filled with getting checked in and helping family members, who arrived throughout the day, check into various hotels, get their credentials, and so on. It's probably similar to getting married when you're excited about seeing family members, but you have to be concerned about the wedding itself in addition to helping them get settled.

There was one neat thing about Thursday night. Our group of about 12 had its first chance to relax together when we went to an Italian restaurant in Cooperstown for dinner. As it turned out, George, his wife Leslie, and two of their boys were seated next to us in this tiny dining room. We had an unplanned, private party. It was a great time with a lot of stories and laughs. While we were sitting there, I offered to buy a round of drinks for the Brett family. A little while later, as the Bretts were leaving, George stood behind my chair, put his hands on my shoulders and announced to the entire Matthews family, "Denny will take care of all of your meals tonight." When our group was finished and ready to leave, I asked the waiter for the bill. He said, "There is no bill. George took care of it." That was a cool and incredible gesture by George.

The four Matthews brothers: (l. to r.) Steve, Doug, Mike and me. When we were growing up, we did everything brothers could think of to do to each other.

Thursday night, I slept hard! I didn't get up Friday morning until about 9:15 or so. Originally, my brothers and I were going to play golf Friday, but a little after 10:00 the weather started turning bad, so we scratched that idea. Instead, I stayed in the room until about noon, finishing my speech for Sunday. Although it'll be similar to the speech I gave at Kauffman Stadium when the Royals honored me with induction into the club's Hall of Fame, I have to make sure that I'm thanking everyone who needs to be recognized for helping me win the Ford Frick Award. The day also consisted of doing TV interviews for ESPN and Metro Sports, and meeting with the Hall of Fame folks about Sunday's ceremony. They have everything timed out carefully because of ESPN's coverage of the event.

Every year, Jane Forbes Clark, who is part of the Singer Sewing Machine family and Chair of the Hall's Board of Directors, invites Hall of Famers and others from baseball to her estate for a huge themed dinner outside. George had told me that one of the highlights of the weekend would be this party. He wasn't kidding. Wow! This year's theme was a "Whale of a party." The tent had a huge balloon whale in the center and then a nautical scene everywhere. The buffet was wonderful. Really, the whole thing was spectacular. I ate dinner with John Schuerholz, former General Manager of both the Royals and the Atlanta Braves. That was a lot of fun. Throughout the evening, I also

The Royals acknowledged my happy news on the crown scoreboard at Kauffman Stadium. What an incredible honor!

had a chance to talk with Reggie Jackson, who had been at Kauffman Stadium earlier this week while the Yankees were in Kansas City, Bill Mazeroski, Harmon Killebrew, who finished his career with the Royals when I was a young broadcaster, and Johnny Bench. Even though I've known these guys for years, it's thrilling to talk with them in this setting, knowing why we're here in Cooperstown.

One interesting conversation I had today was with former Yankee legend Yogi Berra. I had to break the news that Stroud's, the famous chicken restaurant in Kansas City, closed its location out south. Yogi was devastated. When he coached and managed the Yankees during the 1970s and '80s, Yogi made sure he went to Stroud's at least a couple times during a trip to Kansas City. The restaurant would even stay open late to wait for him after a game. (Of course, after a game, while he was waiting on the other coaches, he'd come up to the press room and eat a hot dog right before going to Stroud's for a big meal.) I told Yogi they were trying to find a new location, which prompted him to say, with a chuckle: "If they don't, I'm not coming back to Kansas City." I guess everyone's hoping for a new Stroud's soon.

So, as I mentioned, these first 36 hours or so have been incredibly busy. And incredibly fun. The Hall of Famers are supposed to play golf Saturday morning, assuming the bad weather holds off. I'm not sure who I'm playing with yet, but I'll give you a full report tomorrow.

Saturday, July 28

The Saturday of Hall of Fame weekend consists of three main events: golf, dinner and a closed tour of the Museum.

Because of the weather we've had this weekend, and the fact that it was raining hard when I woke up at 7, I wondered if they'd have the golf tournament. Still, I wandered over to the pro shop at 7:30 and, sure enough, the rain had let up. As the Hall of Famers gather to play, there's a big breakfast buffet outside the pro shop. I again had the opportunity to talk with former Royal Harmon Killebrew and Cincinnati great Johnny Bench. Basically, we sat there for 20 minutes and listened to Johnny tell jokes, which was a blast.

For the tournament, I was paired with Hall of Famers Whitey Ford and Carlton Fisk. The cool thing about it was that my brother Steve's son, Scott, played catcher at Illinois State for three years. Carlton's son was a pitcher and first baseman at ISU during that time. I also knew Carlton a little from his playing days, of course. So those connections, as well as talking about other people we have in common, were a lot of fun.

Whitey Ford, who's 79 now, plays left-handed and can still play golf. He was a lot of fun and talked about the old players he played against. I asked him about the toughest guys for him to get out. He said one of the toughest was Nellie Fox. On the other side of that spectrum, he said he pitched very well against Boog Powell and Jim Gentile, who spent part of his career with the Kansas City A's.

They had the course roped off as if it were a PGA event, and people were lined up all along the way. There were quite a few Boston fans cheering for Fisk. They were big enough fans, evidently, that they traded cigars for autographs. Halfway around the course, some of my family caught us. So I had to tee off among some healthy heckling. Luckily, I hit it right down the middle.

Overall, we had a great time and finished 6-under.

That afternoon, before getting ready for the big dinner, I worked some more on my speech. I think I have it pretty much ready to go. It should be about 10-11 minutes.

Later, they had a reception for the Hall of Famers in one of the rooms here at the hotel. At that time, they announced the winners of the golf tournament and then Dale Petroskey, the President of the Hall of Fame, introduced the four of us who are going in this weekend. It's pretty humbling to have Hall of Fame players applaud when your name is announced. Then, about 7:15, we all went into another room at the hotel for dinner. Cal Ripken, whom I've known since he played, came to our table when things had kind of winded down and shot the breeze for awhile. Although I didn't really know him during his career, I'll add that Tony Gwynn is also a very nice guy, very easy to talk to. By the way, there has been some talk about some Hollywood celebrities being in Cooperstown this weekend. Richard Gere and Linda Carter sat a couple tables over from us at dinner. Those are the only two actors I've seen so far.

After dinner, about 9:30, we were paraded through the streets of Cooperstown in open trolleys, as we made our way to the Hall of Fame Museum. The streets were lined with people 18-20 rows deep. It was relatively dark, so it was an experience to see all the flashbulbs going off as people fired pictures. When we pulled up in front of the museum, all we could see were people. There was a red carpet that led us up to the museum. There was an announcer standing out front announcing the name of each Hall of Famer getting off the trolley. "Please welcome this year's Frick Award winner - Denny Matthews from the Kansas City Royals." People were yelling and screaming. Again, pretty humbling.

We were able to tour the museum privately with our families. I think all of this really hit me for the first time when I went to the broadcasters' and writers' exhibit and saw my picture and a write-up about my career. Of course, we took plenty of pictures with our family, and then

George and his family came up and we took more pictures, and then the Glass family came up and we took some more. That was a lot of fun. As I've mentioned before, it just reaffirms how nice it is to be representing Kansas City and the Royals.

That's me with Tom Cassidy, one of my hockey-playing pals.

As Sunday's ceremony gets closer, I'm feeling the same as I did before a big rivalry game when I played football at Illinois Wesleyan. The anticipation begins on Monday, everything rises throughout the week — the anticipation, adrenaline, butterflies and so on — and it all culminates on game day. In this case, for me, Sunday will be game day.

I just hope I can run a good route and not trip on stage.

Sunday, July 29 – The Big Day

What a weekend! Before I reflect on Sunday's Hall of Fame ceremony and the overall experience of this weekend, as I mentioned in the speech, I just want to thank all of you as fans for your support and encouragement you've shown since I found out in February that I won the Ford Frick Award. I said during Sunday's speech that your hospitality astounds me, and it truly does.

As for Sunday, after getting things packed in the morning and going over my speech one last time, it was time to head to the lobby of the hotel. After mulling around for a little while with my family, the busses of VIPs started heading to the Clark Sports Center for the ceremony. Then, all of the Hall of Famers were taken to a room off the lobby to wait for 25 minutes or so. I got a chance to talk to some of the guys I've known but hadn't seen during the weekend, such as Brooks Robinson, Monte Irvin, Frank Robinson, Tom Seaver — who introduced me on stage — and George Kell. I first met George when he was broadcasting Detroit Tiger games on TV. Even then, he was so encouraging and supportive of both me and my career. Before all of us were taken in two busses to the Clark Sports Center, I made my way toward the door. I could sense someone was to my right. I turned and it was a nice-looking guy, tan, and nicely dressed. It was Sandy Koufax. I introduced myself. He said he'd heard about me, which was incredible. We talked for a few minutes. He's such a soft-spoken, humble person.

Speaking of an incredible conversation, on the bus ride to the induction ceremony, Koufax sat behind me and Willie Mays was next to me. I had heard that Willie was reserved and kind of sullen at times. So that was in my mind when I introduced myself. He turned out to be great. He smiled and shook my hand and proceeded to give me a fascinating conversation over the next 20 minutes. Since I had talked to Monte Irvin, I first asked Willie about Monte as a player.

And then I asked him how he did as a player against Koufax. He said, "Well, I hit four home runs against him and he never threw breaking balls against me. Then one night in San Francisco, late in the year, he threw me a slider and I hit a home run. The next day, I went over and said, 'Sandy, why'd you throw me a slider? You've never thrown me a breaking ball.' Sandy said, 'I wanted to see if you could hit one.'"

After Willie had loosened up talking about Irvin and Koufax, I asked him to tell me about my dad's favorite player, Stan Musial. He said, "Oh, Stan was a wonderful player. He played the game the right way. He was fun to play against. He could play the outfield and first base. We were at the All-Star game, but I can't remember if it was 1954 or '55…somewhere in the mid-1950s. There were just a handful of black players on the National League All-Star team. We didn't really mix and mingle that much with the other guys. We just stayed to ourselves. I remember we were in the clubhouse playing cards, playing poker. None of the other players had come over and said anything to us at all. Even at that time, races didn't mix and mingle that much. But we looked up from our poker game and here came Stan. He pulled up a chair, sat down by us and started to play poker with us." Willie paused for a long time and then said, "Stan didn't know *how* to play poker! But he made us feel more comfortable and made us feel as if we were a part of the National League All-Star team." Then Willie got real serious and said, "I never forgot that. We never forgot that." The thing was, I was thinking how I had never read or heard that story. I started to wonder...am I the only one who's heard that story?

Boy, I wish that ride had been 200 miles instead of 2.

Even though you already know about my speech and the ceremony, there is one neat thing I want to add. When my speech was over and I went back to my seat, the Hall of Famers around me stood up, shook my hand and complimented me on the speech and congratulated me on the award. Imagine Frank Robinson reaching over and shaking your hand and telling you that you did a great job. Man, talk about making you feel good! On top of that, after the ceremony was over, the guys in the back rows and on the other side made it a point to come over and say the same types of things, which I thought was very cool. It's almost as if they're welcoming me into an exclusive club.

Looking back at the entire weekend, I could go back to Cooperstown for the next 20 years and it'd be fun but it'd never be the same as this past weekend. My family wouldn't be there and friends from all over the country wouldn't be there to share in the experience. The induction is unique in that aspect. You get inducted only once. Everybody's there to share it with you only once. No matter how many times you go back, it would be fun but it wouldn't be the same.

What's the expression — "once in a lifetime"? That's a very appropriate cliché to use. I never had experienced anything like that weekend before, and I'll never experience anything like that again. It was an unforgettable experience. It was truly game day. Thank you for sharing it with me.

Leading Into the Speech

Reading back through those "Denny's Diary" entries is a lot of fun for me now because they're more reminders of what a truly remarkable time in my life that was. Now when I sign "HOF 2007" or hear

(l. to r.) That's Dale Petroskey, then-president of the Hall of Fame; my presenter Tom Seaver; me, and Jane Forbes Clark, chair of the Hall's Board of Directors, on the big day.

someone relive that weekend in Cooperstown, it brings back some incredible memories. But, to this day, two years later, I have not watched the DVD of the ceremony or a couple of specials that Kansas City's Metro Sports produced. In fact, it wasn't until working on this book that I looked at some of the gazillion or so photos that I have from that weekend. I figure I'll get to all of that at some point. So, that makes it even more special to read those "Denny's Diary" entries today.

One thing that came to mind as I was reading those was something my broadcast partner at the time, Ryan Lefebvre, did. For some reason, we had a running joke about the Detroit Tigers "Minor League Report" that they release as part of their press packet every Sunday. Through the years, we would come up with unique ways of delivering it to each other. Pretty childish, but we've had fun with it. In 2007, instead of sending him a Christmas card, for instance, I sent him a Tigers Minor League Report. Well, after that incredible bus ride to the ceremony in Cooperstown, we were walking up a ramp toward the stage. Jeff Idelson, who's now the Baseball Hall of Fame President, came running up to me and handed me an envelope. I opened it and inside was the Tigers Minor League Report with a note from Ryan wishing me luck with the speech. That really loosened me up for the speech.

For whatever reason, that year featured two "mosts" — the most ever Hall of Fame members in attendance and the most fans in Cooperstown for Hall of Fame weekend. We just gasped when we stepped on that stage and looked out at the sea of people. We had heard that it was going to be a record crowd, but it was truly amazing.

The previous largest crowd was 1999, the class that included George Brett, when approximately 50,000 people pulled out their blankets and lawn chairs to watch the event. In 2007, the crowd was estimated at 75,000. The majority seemed to be either Orioles or Padres fans.

The only problem that day was the threat of rain and thunderstorms. In case you haven't been to Cooperstown and seen the area around the Clark Sports Center, imagine enough people nearly to fill Arrowhead Stadium, spread out among a couple grassy acres

An estimated 75,000 people attended the Hall of Fame weekend ceremonies in Cooperstown.

with streets that are barely two lanes. So, in hopes of not ending the day in some type of muddy riot, the Hall of Fame folks decided to flip flop the order of the speeches.

Originally, Rick and I were going to be first and second, followed by Tony and Cal. We found out on the bus ride to the ceremony that they decided it would be Tony, Cal, me and then Rick. Hey, lineup changes happen at the last minute in baseball sometimes, and you just adjust and go with it. Even though I mentally had been planning on leading off, I don't mind hitting third behind Tony and Cal. It might've turned out better because I had a chance to sit back, see how the ceremony went, and get a feel for everything.

Before closing the chapter, so to speak, on that weekend in the summer of 2007, it seems appropriate to end this chapter with my actual speech from that day, starting with my thanks to Hall of Fame pitcher Tom Seaver, who introduced me. I'm often asked if I chose Tom for that. I did not. A few years ago, the Hall of Fame decided it would be best for them to choose the person making the introduction. And Tom probably would've been the Hall of Famer I would've picked. George Brett might be the obvious choice, and he would've been super. As with everything George did during his career, he would've worked hard to deliver a great introduction, and he would've come through in the clutch. But in the end, I would've wanted George to sit back and enjoy the festivities. Tom was, well, terrific.

Here we go…

The Speech

Thank you, Tom. Tom Terrific. What a perfect nickname because it fits the person as well as describing the pitcher. Congratulations, Cal, Tony and Rick. And I'm so proud of the fact that all four of us have spent our entire careers with one organization.

Ryan Lefebvre, one of my great broadcasting partners through the years, gave me a secret note that really loosened me up for my Hall of Fame speech.

Ladies and gentlemen, members of the Hall of Fame, today as you bestow upon me the greatest honor a baseball broadcaster can receive, I think back to the 1983 Frick award winner, a childhood hero of mine, Jack Brickhouse. Upon receiving the Frick award, Jack said, "Today, I feel like a man, 60 feet, six inches tall." Half a century, a million memories since I grew up listening to Jack, I tell you what: today I know exactly how he felt.

The summer nights in Bloomington were hot and humid. I'm 10 years old, lying on the living room floor with a big pillow propped up against the big console radio, my baseball cards beside me. I'm listening to the local radio station, WJBC, one of the many stations on the Cardinals radio network, and the voices coming out of that speaker, Joe Garagiola, Jack Buck, Harry Caray, three of the best ever, together talking to me every night. Little did I know, little did they know, but they were preparing and teaching a 10-year-old boy in central Illinois how to broadcast major league baseball. And what marvelous teachers they were. And to think I didn't have to turn in any homework, write any term papers, pay any tuition. I just had to lie in front of the radio each summer night and learn.

At age ten, you don't think about broadcasting. You want to play. And play we did. What beautiful summers they were, pickup games at Fell Avenue Park, Wiffle ball games in the backyard, trading baseball cards with your buddies, then when it grew too dark to play, head to the radio to see how the Cardinals were doing, and when that game was over, spin the radio dial. What other games could I get from far away cities? The quality of the radio signal was immaterial. The opportunity for education irreplaceable, so twist the dial, who do you get? Who's this Ernie Harwell? Boy, he's pretty good. Bob Prince, who does he announce for? I like him. He's funny. Chuck Thompson. (Yeah. I didn't know.) What game is this? I liked to listen to him, too. Maybe when I grow up my voice will be like Chuck Thompson's. You know what? It didn't work out that way.

But still, playing the game is what it's all about. So you play Legion ball and you're fortunate enough to play in high school for John Keegan, and at Illinois Wesleyan University, baseball for Jack Horenberger and football for Don Larson. And you play in summer leagues and then you're lucky enough to get to broadcast some high school and college basketball during your last three years in college. Getting the opportunity to work with two talented professionals like Don Munson and Don Newberg at WJBC Radio while still in college. Great on-the-job training, priceless, invaluable.

Buddy Blattner used to tell me when we started working together that he hated if I wasn't listening while he was doing his innings. He didn't like it if he said something on the air and then I came on and repeated the same thing. "You have to listen to me very carefully and I'm going to be listening carefully to you."

And two years later, with a big assist from Jack Brickhouse, you are hired. Suddenly you're a big league announcer. How in the world did that happen so fast? And when you start out, you're working with one of the best, Buddy Blattner, and what a great teacher he was. More lessons and now you learn to do your homework.

There came a point during my second year, 1970, when I thought my broadcasting career had come to a screeching halt. Now, those of you who listen to big league games, you'll know that every once in a while we have commercial drop-ins, eight or 10 seconds, and you just in-between pitches or between batters drop in a little one-liner. One of our sponsors was a company in Kansas City that made snack foods, potato chips, party nuts, pretzels. They were called Guy's Foods, owned by a nice, little 80-year-old man named Guy Caldwell. We are in Milwaukee; we are coming up on the 4th of July weekend holiday. So I remember the producer handed me a little card that said "Guy's

Foods" so I was supposed to think of a one-liner that would be timely and appropriate and so I said in a burst of brilliance, "For those of you planning a party, make sure you take along plenty of those good Guy's potato chips." It was kind of a slow game and I think Al Fitzmorris, he was about to throw another pitch, and I thought, "You know what, that was pretty good, they are a good sponsor so give it another shot." And the next line out of my mouth was, "And fans, while you're in the store, be sure and grab some Guy's nuts," at which point I thought my budding broadcast career was over. It was going to be back to school and who knows what. You know what, I survived, Guy's Foods survived and here we are 39 years later. And so many people to thank and remember. My father George was an all-American second baseman at Illinois State University and he gave his four sons an awareness and appreciation of the fun and the beauty of the game of baseball. He always encouraged us to play hard, play smart, play well and have fun. The support of a mother Eileen. She never failed to keep dinner warm after a long game or a practice. Three younger brothers, Steve, Doug, Mike, all good athletes, I think, aren't you? All very competitive who, by the way, I dominated in the backyard until all three got bigger, faster and better.

I've had three main broadcasting partners in 39 years. My first partner, the original voice of the Royals, the very talented Buddy Blattner, my coach, my mentor, so helpful, so knowledgeable and so courageous to hire a young guy just out of college with very little broadcasting experience. I couldn't do it without him. Fred White, my partner for 25 years, two guys from central Illinois who had the opportunity to broadcast the most exciting and significant games in Royals history. And now Ryan Lefebvre. We share similar backgrounds; he's a delight to work with. Ryan has a bright future. He will go a long way in the business. And only two producer-engineers in 39 years, that's pretty remarkable, the extremely capable Ed Shepherd and Don Free.

I find it hard to imagine any baseball announcer lucky enough to work for two better team owners, Ewing Kauffman and family and David Glass and family. Remarkable people, wanting only the best for the baseball fans of Kansas City. They are dedicated to that goal, passionate to that end, competing against the big market advantages

Fan's Question:
What do you think is the most impressive feat in baseball – a no-hitter, a triple play, hitting .375 for the season or winning 20 games?

Maddie Stuart
Overland Park, Kansas

Denny: While impressive, a no-hitter and a triple play are from one game. On the flip side, I think hitting .375 for a season and winning 20 games is pretty much a tie. It's really hard to win 20 games, especially these days with so many specialized pitchers in the game and starting pitchers not finishing as many games. Maintaining a level of consistency at the plate to hit .375 or higher has always been less common than 20-game winners. Both are incredibly difficult for their own reasons.

and all the while staying true to their Midwestern values and beliefs. Royals fans are, have been, and will be blessed to have them. David and Ruth Glass, Dan and Penny Glass are here. Thanks for everything.

The Royals have had a succession of excellent general managers, one of them is here today, John Schuerholz from Baltimore. John joined the Orioles organization. And then in 1969, John and I both went to work for the Royals. John, thanks for being here. And I thank so much the friends here from all over the country, great friends from childhood, high school, college and beyond. I'm thrilled and honored that they are here to share in this.

Kansas City has been honored previously here in Cooperstown and I'm so proud to be standing here. Ernie Harwell who stood here in 1984 with our great writer Joe McGuff, who won the Spink award. 1999 George Brett, the first Royals player to go into the Hall of Fame. George, thanks for being here. And just last year my good friend Buck O'Neil, and Buck stood right here. And you know what, folks, if Buck was sitting behind me this afternoon on the platform, I think right about now you'd hear "Oh, yeah, that's right." Buck, we do miss him.

As a baseball broadcaster, I often think about our listeners and I often think about our fans. But wait, aren't they one and the same? Think back to when you were a child when you really started to follow this great game of baseball, and I'm curious, were you a fan who became a listener or were you a listener who became a fan? Either way

I now think of you all as friends and your hospitality really astounds me. You invited my voice into your homes, into your families, into your lives, I know because many of you have told me, in your kitchen, on your patio, in your car, your office, your family room, your basement, you've allowed my voice to ricochet around your garage, fishing boat, you've taken me on picnics and camping trips, but the essence of what a baseball broadcaster does is so well defined in a letter I received

a few years ago from a lady out in Kansas, and bear with me because I've got a tough time getting through this letter.

"Dear Denny, I have loved baseball my whole life. I played softball as a young girl. I have listened to you since the Royals started in 1969. I am 93. I can't do the things I used to do. I can't see very well any more, but that's okay, because I have my radio. So you are my eyes at the ballpark. I don't have to see because you create the picture in my mind with your words. Through your eyes and your words, I feel like I'm sitting at the ballpark watching the game. Listening to the Royals is the highlight of my day. It gives me something to look forward to, so keep up the good work. Sincerely, Margaret Jenkins."

Margaret, I hope you're still listening, because it's folks like you that inspire us to do what we do.

Fans, listeners, friends, my profound thanks to all of you for loving the greatest game in the greatest nation on the face of the earth. Thank you.

Fan's Question: The Royals' families have seen tremendous joy and tears off the field. Are there a couple stories that have shaped you or the organization?

Dana Nearmyer
Olathe, Kansas

Denny: We've lost some great people such as Dick Howser and Dan Quisenberry. Death always has an impact on you. That occurs outside the realm of baseball, too. There's not a big difference between Dick Howser passing away or a good friend passing away, or Mike Sweeney having a baby or a good friend having a baby. Just because it's a baseball person doesn't add or take away from the trauma or sadness or joy that you feel. People in the organization, such as Mr. Kauffman, have shaped me, but not necessarily out of joy or tears.

CHAPTER TWO
On the Road Again

I 've never really sat down and tried to figure out how many road trips I've taken with the Royals or even how many games I've seen on the road. Well into the thousands.

When I first joined the Royals in 1969, it was a great thrill to travel around the American League. The cities were new to me, so I was doing touristy things that I'd never done before, for the most part. Also, at that time, I was about the same age as many of the players. So we hung out quite a bit on the road. As time went on, the newness wore off and I got older. These days, with all due respect that a country music fan like me would give Willie Nelson, I probably *can* wait to get on the road again.

One person providing many stories throughout this chapter is David Witty, who was with the Royals for 21 years, 15 of which were spent as the traveling secretary. During his time in those 15 years, he never missed a road trip. Even during those other six years, he didn't miss many.

It's people like Dave, the traveling secretary, who helps keep a Major League team moving from city to city. When you think about all of the trips teams in the Major Leagues take throughout a season, it's pretty incredible to realize that teams always reach their destinations and they do so safely.

That's not to say that there isn't the occasional rough flight. We had one in the 1980s coming back from Seattle that was the worst one ever. It was just unbelievable. There was a line of thunderstorms going west to east across the country. Since Seattle is north of Kansas City, the pilot went parallel with the storm as far as he could before heading south. Once he went south, the flight experience seemed to be heading in that same direction because there was no way to get under or over or around this storm, so he had to fly through it. It was about 25 minutes of the brightest lightening, hard rain, and just bumping around that we've ever been through. It was easily the worst, bumpiest, most frightening ride we've ever had.

There was another time that was more memorable than scary. We were headed to Chicago and we had to abort coming in for a landing. Basically, we were about 1,000 feet off the deck, but we were long on final approach, so the pilot went full throttle on the engines and we went straight up. Another plane just hadn't cleared the runway yet and the tower told our pilot to make another pass. So, instead of going down, you suddenly start going up. I knew what was happening so I wasn't worried, but if you don't know what's happening you might be concerned.

DAVID WITTY: "Coming into Kansas City in the summer is interesting because of the thunderstorms. There always seemed to be a few flights a year that were white knucklers. Although I think most flights were white knucklers for pitchers Mark Gubicza and Luis Aquino, who didn't do well with flying. Two happenings, landing-wise, come to mind. The first was one year we were scheduled to leave but we were delayed getting on the Braniff flight because the pilot ran the plane off the runway before we got in it. Another time we were going from Boston to Chicago on a Sunday on this incredibly beautiful charter plane through MGM Grand Air. It was an incredible plane inside, completely decked out. I don't know if Elvis or the President fly in such luxury. That didn't make our landing in Chicago any smoother. The runway at Midway isn't long, and as we landed, it felt as if the plane just dropped into the asphalt. I thought we went through the runway. I've never been on a flight with a harder landing. Those two jump out the most.

"Another one that stands out was in late July, shortly after the All-Star break, in 1988. We had lost four in a row, after losing a series finale in New York and then being swept in Detroit. We got on the bus to head to the airport and it wasn't air conditioned. So, we've lost four in a row, it's July and we're on this non-air conditioned bus. When we got out to the airport, we had to hurry because thunderstorms were moving in, so we had a small window in which to leave. We got on our Midwest Express plane, which was small anyway, and got settled. The crew was trying to hurry us along, telling everyone to sit down. For whatever reason, Willie Wilson wouldn't sit down. He was the only one standing. George Brett starts yelling at Willie to sit down. They got into a scuffle that was broken up by pitcher Steve Farr and coach Adrian Garrett. The FCC and airport security had to come on board. That caused us to miss our window to leave and we ended up sitting on the runway for at least two hours waiting on the thunderstorms to pass. During this time, they shut the plane off, so now we've lost four games in a row, we went to the airport in a non-air-conditioned bus and we're sitting on a runway in a smaller, non-air-conditioned plane. That was quite an ordeal."

Planes, Trains and, Well, Busses

As you may know from listening to broadcasts, I'm a big fan of trains. It's a fascination I've had all my life. During the 1990s, Witty, largely in an effort to keep costs down and as something different, booked a couple of train trips, instead of flights, between cities on our east coast road trip. We went from Boston to New York a couple of times and Baltimore to New York. We had two chartered coaches, one for sitting and one a dining car. One of the Boston to New York trips made a stop in Hartford, Connecticut. We had a diesel-powered engine from Boston to Hartford, and an electric engine from Hartford to New York City. I sat in the cab from Boston to Hartford. The engineer was a female and she was not happy with the equipment.

"This goat is stuck on 96 and I can't get it to go any faster," she kept saying, along with a few choice curse words, as we whistled along. She wasn't real happy with it, but I certainly wasn't complaining.

DAVID WITTY: "Those were fun to do especially when I looked at the time schedules. It was basically as fast to do it that way as it would've been to fly. Besides, we could stay off the commercial flights and spend about $4,000 for the train trip instead of $20,000 to fly. It was relaxing for the players and probably a new experience for most of them. Writer Dick Kaegel, who used to travel by train to some of the Major League cities early in his career, would talk about the cigars they smoked and the brandy they drank. So, our experience was like an old-time baseball train trip. It took us back to a different era in baseball. No other teams, as far as I know, did it during the time I was in baseball, and no one does it today. It was worth it, though."

When we played in Washington D.C. against the Senators, we stayed at the Shoreham Hotel, which was about a 30-minute ride to the ballpark. That is, if you didn't have our bus driver this one time.

We played on a Saturday afternoon, and after the game we were on the bus headed back to the hotel. We pulled up to an intersection, and I noticed a barbershop named Shorty's on the corner. After another 10 minutes, there was another corner barbershop named Shorty's. It looked similar to the first, but no big deal. Then, another one. Ed Shepherd, our radio producer-engineer, said, "Man, this Shorty must be doing pretty well because he has a chain of barbershops all over town."

Shorty might've had a slew of shops around town, but we saw only one. The bus driver was lost and had been driving in circles.

Put Me In, Coach

This might surprise some people, but I actually played in six or seven exhibition games for the Royals in the 1970s, while Whitey Herzog was managing the club. Whitey put me in right field, left field, and at third base a couple of times. Even though I played second base in college, I never got a chance to in those exhibition games. I'm not complaining, though.

In 1978, we were playing an in-season exhibition game at the U.S. Naval Academy. We were in Baltimore and we had two days off. The

Royals played a series in Toronto that finished on Tuesday, and then had until Friday before playing the Orioles. Whitey wanted to have a workout one day and play a game the other day, so he scheduled the Naval Academy team. We went to the Naval Academy and spent the entire day there. It's only about a 40-minute drive from Baltimore.

We went over about 8:30 in the morning, got a tour of the Naval Academy when we first got there, and then we had lunch with all of the Midshipmen at Bancroft Hall. Each one of us sat at a table with the Midshipmen, which was cool. After lunch we finished our tour and then went over and got dressed for the game.

They had a neat ballpark, similar to Wrigley Field around home plate and down the lines. We played Navy. There was a guy there from WIBW in Topeka doing a documentary on traveling with the Royals. While he was recording, I drew a walk. At the urging of first-base coach Freddie Patek, I stole second base. I then went to third on U.L. Washington's groundball to second, and then Jerry Terrell hit a fly ball to center, which scored me. So, if I ever need it, I have proof, I guess. That was cool, though. I also have video from our tour. I don't remember a person ever traveling with us at any other time to record the team on the road, so I'm fortunate that he happened to be on that trip.

I played the outfield that day. Whitey put the bench guys in their spots first and then he put me wherever he needed another body. It was common knowledge at that time that if there was an exhibition game, I was going to play.

As Whitey used to tell me, "With you on the field, I know one of my regular players won't get hurt." That was his theory. It didn't matter if I got hurt, I could still go up to the booth and talk.

Playing in those games helped give me credibility with the players because I came down out of the booth to their place of work, literally. The players then figured that I had some credibility in describing a difficult play, or saying that a ball took a crappy hop, or saying that a player should have fielded that ground ball. Actually, it was a no-lose situation for me because I obviously hadn't been playing or practicing. If I did anything positive, that's a plus. But the pressure for me was not to embarrass myself. Things worked out OK. Needless to say, putting on the uniform and playing was a thrill for me, and it gave the players somebody to needle.

When we played the Naval Academy, they didn't know all of our guys, obviously, and they thought I was one of the players. When one of the Royals told a Navy player that I was the broadcaster, he wasn't totally buying it — but I was definitely a non-roster participant.

Charley Lau was the batting instructor at the time for the Royals, but he didn't make the trip to Annapolis. By the time we got back to our hotel in Baltimore, Charley was in the lobby and had heard about that day's exhibition. He walked up to me and his face broke into the little Charley Lau grin. He said, "I hear you did OK." That was it. That made me feel about 14 feet tall. What a great day! Out of all the jobs in baseball, playing is still the best and the most fun. I'm appreciative that Whitey gave me the opportunity to revisit my youth.

That night, we went to Bo Brooks, which was the place in Baltimore where we'd always go for crabs. Marty Pattin's son, Jon, made a trip with us. Jon was probably around 7 years old or so. At this restaurant, they'd bring us pitchers of beer and plates full of crabs for the table. I don't know if Marty gave Jon a little sip of beer or what, but after about 45 minutes of all of us eating crabs and drinking beer, "Pflatt!" Jon fell off his chair. Marty looked at Jon and in his best Donald Duck impression, said, "Did you have too much beer, Jon?"

During the 2008-09 off season, I heard a story about another trip to Baltimore that I hadn't heard before. I was on one of the Royals Caravan trips with a few guys, including Willie Wilson. He told me a wonderful story about a game in Baltimore against the Orioles in 1989, during Jamie Quirk's 25-game career with the O's.

WILLIE WILSON: "My nickname when I played was 'bean.' We were playing Baltimore and I was leading off. Jamie Quirk, by that time, was catching for the Orioles. I'm walking to the plate and Jamie starts, 'Bean, Bean, Bean. What's going on?' I said, 'Not much, Q, what about you?' He said, 'OK, Bean, here comes a fastball.' I didn't believe him...phfft! Right down the middle. 'Be quiet, Q, stop talking!' 'OK, Bean, here comes another fastball.' I didn't believe him again...phfft! Right down the middle. Now I'm really yelling at him to shut up. 'OK,

Bean here comes another fastball.' I swung and missed. It was a curveball. Strike three. I looked at him and he just started laughing. He was funny with a dry sense of humor. I heard him laughing, though, my entire way back to the dugout."

When I mentioned that to Quirk, he grinned, shrugged his shoulders and said, "Yeah, I'm not sure why Willie didn't believe me."

Garbonzo!

Former pitcher Mark Gubicza is one of my favorite Royals. He was one of the favorites of his teammates, and one of the important pieces of the puzzle for the Royals in the 1980s.

The first time you're looking at his name, Gubicza's name reads like an eye chart. During spring training we went to Pompano Beach to play Texas. Pompano Beach had the oldest, rickety ballpark. It was made completely of wood, and it looked like it was tipping. Not exactly the best place to be in the press box if the stadium fell.

The press box was on top of this old deck, and it would sway in the wind. Our booth was tiny, with the public address announcer in the booth next to us. The partition between us was a thin piece of plywood, not much thicker than construction paper. Gubie, a rookie nobody had really heard of yet, was starting that day. About 10 minutes before the game, the PA guy stuck his head in the door, said, "I think I got all your guys' names down, but how do you pronounce this pitcher's name?" I pronounced it for him. He practiced a few times while he stood there, but he just could not pronounce Gubicza. He went back to his little room and Fred White and I could hear him practicing. A couple of minutes before the game, the PA guy goes over the lineup over the loud speaker. He gets to Gubie: "And pitching for the Royals, Mark Garbonzo." Then, *CLICK*, our PA friend shut off his microphone and started cussing at his inability to pronounce Gubie's name. Fred and I were laughing so hard that we had trouble going on the air. So much for 10 minutes of practice and my excellent pronunciation lesson.

But, anybody who has known Gubie, just loves him. He's a wonderful person.

GEORGE BRETT: "He was a shy, quiet guy. He lived with me the first month of the season (in 1984), when no one expected him to make the club out of spring training. No one expected Bret Saberhagen to make the club out of spring training in 1984. When they did make the club, obviously they needed a place to stay. Instead of putting them in a hotel near the ballpark, which is where they put everyone back then, I had two extra bedrooms in my house. I said, 'You guys need a place to stay, why don't you stay with me until you find a place to live.' They stayed with me for the first month because they weren't in a hurry to find a place to live. Finally, I called people I knew to get them out of the house. [Laughs]

"After about three weeks, Gubie asked me one day if he could use the phone and get something to eat from the refrigerator. I said, 'Mark, you can use the phone any time you want to and you can eat anything out of the refrigerator that you want.' Meanwhile, Saberhagen would come down first thing in the morning, go raid my closet, put on my clothes and take off. Gubicza was the complete opposite, just a quiet, shy guy. I remember getting up many late mornings and I'd hear a clanging noise upstairs. It was Mark lifting weights. He was a dedicated, devoted athlete. … He lifted weights every morning before he went to the ballpark. He did 2,000 sit-ups a day in his room. You always saw him doing something. He wasn't a couch potato kind of guy. He was doing whatever he could to improve himself everyday."

One guy who I can guarantee didn't lift weights and do 2,000 sit-ups a day was Steve Mingori, who pitched for the Royals during the 1970s. Mingo was someone I hung out with quite a bit. Mingo, who passed away in 2008, was a beauty.

When you think about a baseball clubhouse and guys hurling wonderful insults at one another, you can think of Mingo, who had some great lines and, um, interesting thoughts.

STEVE MINGORI: "Jim Colborn, what a beauty he was. He threw a no-hitter (in 1977). He came out in the paper and predicted he'd throw another one in Milwaukee, which is where he used to play. I was the bullpen captain and I sarcastically told the guys we didn't need to go to the bullpen because Colborn promised to throw a no-hitter. But, I told them if I thought he had his stuff, we'd stay in the dugout. If he didn't, we'd go to the bullpen. Colborn threw about four pitches in the game and I told them that we needed to go. So, at that moment, we all made a mad rush to the bullpen.

"We always had a great time in the bullpen. (At home), we had hot plates in there and a pay phone. We'd cook kielbasas out there. The short relievers would eat in the first three innings and the long relievers would eat after the sixth inning. We'd call our girlfriends or our wives and talk to them during the game. We didn't have a lot of talent in the bullpen but we had a lot of guts and a lot of pride. When Marty Pattin would lose a game, he'd bust out every light bulb in the hallway — I'd come in and hear a POP! POP! POP! He took his shoe off one time and threw it toward the roof. He never found that shoe.

"Then we had Al Hrabosky. The first time I met him, we went to dinner with his wife and my girlfriend on the Plaza. There was a rose there with thorns. He ate all of it, thorns and all. He later asked me if I'd help him with his changeup, which I did. It was funny because he'd go (behind the mound) for his fist pump and his mad stare, and he'd stomp up to the mound. And then he'd throw a changeup. He was a beauty."

Al Hrabosky, the Mad Hungarian, once ate the rose on a restaurant table, thorns and all.

Really, they had some talent in the bullpen and, in those days, the guys were very close, especially Mingo, Marty and Doug Bird. There was a time, however, when the relievers felt as if they weren't getting the attention they deserved. We were in Cleveland and it was cold. They were having a bat give-away day. At that time, Cleveland wasn't drawing well but they had about 30,000 people there that day. Well, Mingo took white tape and formed the letter "B" on the back of one of the pitcher's blue warm-up jackets. Then, he took the tape and made a "U" on somebody else's jacket. Eventually, from the tallest player to the shortest, they spelled out "BULLPEN." Then, he had all the guys come out of the dugout at the same time and walk toward the right-field bullpen.

Speaking of Cleveland, our buddy Al Fitzmorris tells a wonderful story from his time spent playing for the Indians, 1977-78.

AL FITZMORRIS: "Phil Seghi was the Cleveland general manager, who was just a blow-hard. At the time I'm with International Management Group, maybe the first baseball player they had. They also had Jack Nicklaus, Tom Weiskopf, and people like that. I was their experiment and it wasn't going well. My wife Jan and I went back to Cleveland and we stayed there. I went to the caravan, no contract. They called me back one more time and I said, 'If I don't have a contract by the time I leave, that's it, I'm done.' It was freezing cold then in Cleveland. They had some foreign ship that was frozen in the lake and probably wasn't going to get out for three months. Serious cold. Everything was going wrong. So we're headed into the last negotiations and I told my agents, 'Let me handle this.' We went in and sat down, and I said, 'Phil, it's obvious that you're not that interested in having me as a player.' They had traded their No. 1 catcher, Alan Ashby, for me. I said, 'Here's the deal. I want three years and (this figure). You know what? I'm even looking at housing. But I can't buy anything because I don't have a contract. I'm not making any money. Unless I sign a contract, I'm not buying a house.'

Seghi said, 'You're actually looking for property?' 'Yeah.' 'Alright, let's do it.' So I signed this contract, and as I started to walk out he said, 'By the way, where have you been looking?' I said, 'Alpine.' 'Where's Alpine?' I said, 'It's just east of San Diego.' He said, 'You're not going to live in Cleveland?' I gave him a funny look and said, 'No way, who in the world would live in Cleveland?' He just started screaming at me. My agents are dying, they're laughing so hard. But you know what? We had a signed contract. That's pretty much how my career went in Cleveland."

Oh, Wolfy

Outfielder Jim Wohlford was an easy guy to pick on. He was unwittingly funny. But, he always took other people's ribbings in good humor. Wohlford platooned in left field most of the time, but he was a good contact hitter who could run.

One year during spring training, before he had made the Royals roster, he put himself in an awkward situation. Of course, in early spring training there are so many guys that aren't going to make the club. He used to say to me from time to time, "Denny, Jim Wohlford can hit." "Yeah, yeah, I know, Wolfy, you can hit." But this one day in Fort Myers, he was in the group that was taking batting practice. There must have been eight or 10 guys in his group, which means each player's only getting five or six swings and maybe a bunt. In that situation, it was tough for everyone to get good work.

I was standing next to the batting cage and Wolfy gets his five or six hacks, and he comes out of the batting cage. I could tell he was a little bit irritated. (Keep in mind, Jim Wohlford was one of the nicest guys on the team. I never heard him say a bad thing about anyone.) He said, "Boy, I can't wait until we get some of the deadwood out of here," meaning some of the minor-league guys, "so we can get some more swings."

Sure enough, the next morning, some of that "deadwood" was on the bus headed to the minor-league camp at Sarasota … including Jim Wohlford.

Once he made the Royals, he had at least one memorable at-bat. We were playing a game at Yankee Stadium. Late in a close game, Wolfy hit a ball in the gap in left-center and started running. And running. He wheeled around to third for a triple. Out of the dugout came New York manager Billy Martin, who protested that Wolfy missed second base. The umpire ruled him out. Whitey Herzog was enraged! And he came charging out of the dugout, heading for the umpire. First-base coach Steve Boros cut Whitey off before he reached the umpire.

"Whitey, before you go out there to argue, there's something you should know."

"What?"

"Wolfy missed first base, too."

Whitey didn't say another thing. He turned right around and headed back to the dugout. That was Wolfy.

Minnesota: Land of 10,001 Lakes if You Count Ducky's Suit

I first came across Marty Pattin when we were in high school. We played baseball against each other all through school, American Legion ball, and then in college.

Marty was a hard thrower, who came right over the top with a lot of high fast balls and an occasional little breaking ball. He stayed healthy throughout his career, but he fought his weight. He loved to eat. There are countless stories about how Ducky would irritate some poor waitress because he used his Donald Duck impression to order his meal.

Marty decided to try a rubber warm-up suit and run in the outfield before games to bring his weight down. We were in Minnesota — in the Twins' old stadium — and it was hot and humid. Marty was running in the outfield and he dehydrated and collapsed. It was a scary situation because, obviously, it wasn't known at that time that he was dehydrated. An ambulance came and rushed him to the hospital. The players were absolutely stunned by it.

Unfortunately, it was before the first game of a double-header. I don't remember the outcome of the game, but I do remember that everyone was worried about Marty during that first game. Between games, everyone went into the clubhouse to see if they could find something out about Marty's condition while they replenished their own energy. Well, no need to worry about Ducky. When the guys got in there, Ducky was putting a dent in the food spread. Evidently, he recovered nicely from his dehydration.

Another of the funniest things I saw during any game happened in Minnesota. Fellow central Illinois guy Kevin Seitzer, who became the hitting coach for the Royals before the 2009 season, was known for his hitting, but he also was a solid defensive player. Unfortunately, there's one play that many people remember. Of course, it doesn't hurt that it made the blooper reels for years. I'll set it up by saying that there were runners on first and second with no outs and Dan Gladden, the Twins' speedy outfielder, was at the plate. I'll let Seitz, who was playing third base that day, take it from here.

KEVIN SEITZER: "We had the number-one play bunt defense on, which meant that the third baseman was supposed to read it. If it was a good bunt, we'd go get it. If it was a bad bunt, we'd go back and cover third. Gladden could fly. When he laid (the bunt) down, it was one of those that was perfect, six inches from the foul line, rolling perfectly parallel with no spin. It was going to stay fair. I came bolting in, and I have this flashback to a highlight I remember of a guy with the Mariners way back when, getting down on his hands and knees, and blowing the ball foul. So I do this hook slide next to the ball, and I'm doing an army crawl as fast as I can, blowing as hard as I can. Unfortunately, it was brand new turf so it was very rigid. It wasn't slick at all. That ball just came to a stop, fair. I looked up and the umpire says, 'Son, what in the (world) are you doing?' I told him I was trying to get the ball foul. He said, 'You can't do that, they changed the rule!' Oh, man. I made an idiot out of myself for no reason."

Why Does Everything Happen in Milwaukee?

A great city, but one of the oddest in terms of things that have happened on road trips, is Milwaukee. On and off the field, it's been the site for some interesting moments.

The Royals greatest comeback happened in Milwaukee, actually, on Friday night, June 15, 1979. We had a day game scheduled for Saturday afternoon, so when the Royals got down by nine runs in about the fourth inning, 11-2, Whitey Herzog took his starters out of the lineup and told them to go back to the hotel and get a good night's sleep: "We'll get 'em tomorrow afternoon."

Of course, as it turned out, the subs rallied, made up the nine-run difference and added three more for good measure, and won 14-11.

There was a lounge right off the main lobby at our hotel, the Pfister. When we all got off the bus back at the hotel after the game, around 11 p.m., the guys who went back early to get a good night's sleep were sitting in the lounge swapping stories and having a few adult beverages. As we entered the hotel, one of the guys getting off the bus announced: "We don't need you guys, we won!"

"Sure you did! Real funny."

It took a lot of convincing before the starters believed they actually missed the greatest comeback in club history.

DAVID WITTY: "My first road trip as traveling secretary with the Royals was to Milwaukee. We took an Eastern Airlines commercial flight to Milwaukee and then city busses picked us up at the airport. It was one of those accordion style busses, that's basically two busses with the accordion-looking connecter between the two. That bus (or busses, however you want to look at it) took us to the Pfister Hotel, which was an old, dark hotel that they've since remodeled and added on to. Of course, the Brewers were playing in County Stadium at the time, which wasn't a great stadium. So, you think about traveling with a Major League team as being glamorous, but that first trip was anything but. And we're talking about 1987. Not that long ago.

"There was a rumor that the Pfister Hotel had ghosts. I had a player's wife and a player — unrelated and in different years — both claim to have seen this ghost on the eighth floor of the hotel, in room 810, I think. Pitcher Tom Gordon, who was 19 and naïve when he came up, knew about the ghost in Milwaukee. He'd say, 'Don't put me on the eighth floor, Witty, don't put me there. I'm not there, am I?' I'd look at the room assignments and say, 'Yep, I think you're on the eighth floor.' We'd go back and forth because he absolutely didn't want to stay on the eighth floor because of the haunted rumors.

"Something always seems to happen in Milwaukee. When the Brewers played their games at County Stadium, we had games delayed because of floods. We've had a couple power outages at the new stadium, Miller Park. One of those happened in June 2001, and the game was postponed. The next day, Royals pitcher Blake Stein went out and struck out 11 Brewers, including eight in a row, but the Royals lost 5-2. We've also had floods and a snowstorm there. I'm not sure what it is about Milwaukee."

Bo Does Everything

As anyone will tell you, Bo Jackson was the greatest athlete ever for the Royals. He was also one of the best players around kids that I have ever seen. He related to kids beautifully. They loved him. Even though he could be intimidating to adults, he had an incredible ability to make little kids feel at ease.

On the field, the speed that Bo could generate and the power that he could generate as a hitter were the two things that really stood out. After signing Bo, the Royals brought him to Kansas City for batting practice, before he was to report in the minor leagues at Memphis. It was obvious that Bo had "easy power" — he would swing smoothly and the ball just kept going. A lot of guys hit the ball hard, it goes for a ways, and then it begins to descend. When Bo made contact, the ball kept carrying.

JOHN SCHUERHOLZ: "Bo is the greatest athlete I have ever seen in a baseball uniform. He could hit a ball farther, throw a ball farther, and run faster than any human being I have ever seen in a baseball uniform. It was a coup for us to sign Bo Jackson."

KEVIN SEITZER: "Bo was the greatest talent of any athlete I've ever seen. Every day you went to the ballpark, you had a chance to see something you had never seen before. ... I was in the same (batting practice) group as Bo, Frank White and George Brett. Every day in BP, Bo would turn around and swing left-handed for his last pitch. He had a terrible swing left-handed, but he was so strong and his hands were so quick. Usually he'd pop the ball up in the cage or beat it into the ground in front of home plate. We were in Minnesota and in right-centerfield, on the facing of the third deck, there was a Dairy Queen sign. Bo turned around in batting practice and swung left-handed. He connected with a ball that was so loud and went so far, it ended up hitting that Dairy Queen sign. It was the most amazing thing I think I saw in my whole career.

"In 1986, Bo and I were both called up in September. He hit a home run off Mike Moore and I will never, ever forget the sound that that bat made when it hit the ball. The ball landed up on the hill, by the highway, and they measured it at something like 550 feet. We were sitting in the dugout up on the seat, and we had to get down off the seat and look up because the trajectory was so high that the ball went out of vision from the seat in the dugout. It was absolutely incredible."

DAVID WITTY: "Traveling with Bo was like traveling with the Rolling Stones or U2 or something. We'd get off the bus and everywhere we went people would be lined up, yelling for him. One of my greatest nights on the road was in July 1990, when we were in New York to play the Yankees. Bo hit three home runs in the game off Andy Hawkins, and got seven RBIs. In the bottom of the sixth inning, Bo's two-sport counterpart, Deion Sanders, hit an inside-the-park home run to centerfield. On that play, Bo dove for the ball in center, separated his shoulder and had to go to the hospital. (Willie Wilson replaced him during the inning.) Bo was due up fourth the top of the next inning. One more home run, which would've been possible for Bo, would've tied Lou Gehrig's record for home runs in a game at Yankee Stadium. Could you imagine? Since I was also on the road as the PR guy, trainer Nick Swartz called me from the hospital to tell me that Bo had a subluxation of his right shoulder. The PR guy announces over an intercom to the press box what's going on with the team. So, I went on the intercom at Yankee Stadium and made the announcement. I was about 27 at the time, and I'm making an announcement at Yankee Stadium about an athlete who's had this incredible game. Meanwhile, all these writers are yelling for me to spell subluxation. It was incredible to witness that performance by Bo."

When I think about Bo, I think about power and speed. The power he generated with his bat, which resulted in some incredible home runs, and the time he hit the bottom of the crown scoreboard at Kauffman Stadium. And I think about his incredible running speed. When you talk to scouts about running speed from home to first, they'll tell you that the left-handed hitters get to first faster because they're a hair closer. Bo, a right-handed hitter, could make a routine ground ball to the left side of the infield a very close play at first base.

DAVID WITTY: "We used to keep a sheet on a legal pad — I think I still have it — listing the dates and all the things that Bo did on the field. There was that three home-run night in Yankee Stadium. The night in Seattle when he threw out Harold Reynolds. The night he ran up the wall in Baltimore. When he broke the bat over his knee and the night he finished breaking an already-cracked bat over his head. George Brett is the only other player the Royals have had with all the incredible feats.

"Bo and I had a good relationship. I was always Witty to him. From a traveling and PR standpoint, I never had any problems with him. He liked to play the intimidation card with people, but I got along with him fine. I was a huge Raiders fan, so one year I decided I wanted him to sign a football that I could add to my collection. The only thing was that he wouldn't sign footballs during the baseball season. I'd ask every now and again, and he'd always say no, not during the season. Finally, on the last day of the season we were in Oakland, and I took the football to him in the clubhouse after the final out. As he signed it, he started laughing because he made me wait all year long."

It's a shame that things didn't turn out better with his hip. He was on his way to an amazing baseball career.

Fan's Question:
Do you think baseball owners should bring back more doubleheaders?

Tim Brown
Overland Park, Kansas

Denny: It's obvious that the reason for a lack of doubleheaders is the fact that it's two games for the price of one. As salaries have skyrocketed, teams realize the need to maximize what they're making. I don't think you draw many more fans for a doubleheader anymore. When doubleheaders were common and popular, games were a lot shorter. If you had a doubleheader that started at 1 p.m., you'd be done by 6 or so. Today, you're probably still there at 8:30 at night. I think it would be cool, though, to have one scheduled Sunday afternoon or holiday double-header a year as opposed to a forced one because of a postponed game.

Sprint

CHAPTER THREE
Kauffman Stadium Memories

oyals Stadium. Kauffman Stadium. The K. Whatever you call it, it's still the magical place that the Royals have called home since 1973, after spending their first four seasons at Municipal Stadium. It was wonderful when it opened, but the changes it has undergone, including the massive facelift before the 2009 season, make it an incredible home.

The stadium has been the site of some unforgettable moments, many of which you'll read about throughout this book. Others, you won't. Simply put, as Matt wrote in the book's introduction, there are plenty of articles, books and videos that cover the great games at Kauffman Stadium: the great rivalry games with the Yankees, including the play-offs. The postseason series against the Toronto Blue Jays. George Brett eclipsing the .400 mark. The two World Series, 1980 and '85. And so on.

You know about the games. For instance, most Royals fans know everything they need to know about the "Pine Tar Game" at Yankee Stadium on July 24, 1983. And, people even realize now that the Pine Tar Game actually started a couple of weeks earlier, when New York manager Billy Martin noticed when they were in Kansas City that George had pine tar above the label on his bat. Of course, when you protest in baseball, you want to do it at a time when it could benefit you. George didn't do anything in that series in Kansas City to help the

45

Royals win, so the Yankees kept it inside their jacket pockets because they knew the Royals were going to be at Yankee Stadium a couple of weeks later. Many, if not most, fans know that now.

Since you know about many of the games, I won't re-hash them here. At least not many. My bigger fascination has been with the stadium.

Originally, the Royals were supposed to move into their new digs in 1972, the same year the Chiefs moved into Arrowhead. Only problem was a construction strike that caused a delay. As I recall, though, groundskeeper George Toma dug up home plate in a ceremony of sorts after the Royals final home game at Municipal in 1971. It was supposed to symbolize the move from old to new. A big deal was made about hauling home plate over to the new yard. Instead, he was whacking it back into the ground of Municipal in 1972, right where he dug it up about six months earlier. They did the same thing the following year.

Once construction resumed during that winter, the crew had a 22-year-old by the name of Frank White. Yes, *that* Frank White, the same one who thrilled us for 18 seasons and has a statue at the stadium now.

Frank White was the first – and best – graduate of the innovative Royals Baseball Academy.

At the time, Frank had just finished playing Class AA ball for the Royals.

FRANK WHITE: "I did labor stuff, carried things here and there. When they poured the columns for the main level, I had this little machine, and I'd drive around and smooth out the concrete that ran over. On the third floor, I learned how to seal some bathroom floors."

Kauffman Stadium opened in April 1973. At that time, the stadium was very stark. There was no color. When you looked to the outfield, there was no signage of any kind, nor any plants or bushes on the terrace. The scoreboard was as far as the outfield went. Still, it was beautiful.

The only complaint I had, though, was that they used artificial turf. In fact, I made the statement on the air that night that if there were grass on this field, Royals Stadium (its name at the time) would be a perfect Major League Baseball stadium. I understood the club's reasoning behind the turf, thinking they'd be able to guarantee — for the most part — that most games would be played, so if you're traveling from Wichita or Salina or Omaha, you'd still see a game. Well, obviously, that didn't exactly work out as planned. There were postponements because they didn't have the drain-through artificial turf. So, when it rained, it took the grounds crew nearly an hour to squeegee the field.

Not to mention the fact that the Royals had the best groundskeeper in all of sports in George Toma. Why waste him on turf?

GEORGE TOMA: "I didn't care (if the surface was artificial turf or natural grass), because I had worked with both in the Super Bowls. Whatever they wanted to do, it was up to them to do. A lot of people wanted natural grass. There were bumper stickers out there that said, 'Let George do it.' But they chose 3M Tartan Turf. They told me to make a punch list of things that needed to be fixed. I thought, 'No, way. I'm a natural grass man, so they'll think I'm just messing around.' So I told them what they needed to do was have Mrs. Muriel Kauffman, Mr. Cedric Tallis' wife, Charlie Truett's wife, and all the girls in the office go down there and make the checklist. I said, 'There aren't enough coffee tables in Kansas City to cover up the bad spots.' They had me do it anyway, so I got the boys from Lincoln, Paseo and Central to come out and put duct tape wherever they used to put sand and seed to fix divots. They had over a thousand pieces of duct tape out there. 3M and the architects made fun of us because they didn't think we knew what we were talking about. They made us feel so small. But we had the last laugh because six months later, 3M had to come in, take the entire base out, the entire carpet out, and put a new one in at their own expense.

"The secret to all of it is the installation. Even the second installation, the Astroturf, at Royals Stadium was bad. (The Royals) should've never accepted it. The architects and the contractors have to do a good job. The first thing you have to do is think of the players. You have to have a good playing surface for the preschool kids all the way up to the professionals, because the cheapest insurance for an athlete is a good, safe playing field."

The same architect who designed stadiums for the Dodgers and the Angels designed Royals Stadium. They took the best of Dodger Stadium, eliminated the few mistakes they made, and put it into Anaheim Stadium. Then they took Anaheim Stadium, eliminated any mistakes they felt they had, and that became Royals Stadium.

The stadium opened officially on April 10, 1973, when the Royals played host to the Texas Rangers, who were managed by Whitey Herzog. It was an extremely cold night, temperature around 39 degrees, but the Royals played a terrific game.

During that first game, which the Royals won 12-1, Big John Mayberry took home the honors of hitting the first home run. Mayberry, who was the Royals first power hitter, knocked out the last homer in Municipal Stadium in 1972 before reaching his goal of being the first with a home run at the new ballpark.

JOHN MAYBERRY: "That first home run at Royals Stadium, I thought about it all winter long. I said I gotta be the first to hit one out. I didn't want Freddie Patek to hit one out, I didn't want Amos Otis to hit one out, I didn't want some Texas Rangers guy to hit one out. About the fifth inning I caught one and hit it out. It was real cold, opening day. Splittorff got the win. We blew them out on our way to a great season that year.

"I lost a few home runs, but we won more games with the Astroturf. It was a great place to play. It was beautiful, and it's still beautiful, even more so with the (renovations). I really enjoyed my days, except for maybe those hot days in July and August when the temperature on that turf was about 130 or 140 degrees. But we got through it and we had a great team and a great time."

About three months later, the baseball world got its introduction to the Royals' new home, when Kansas City hosted the All-Star Game.

All of my family was here from Illinois to see the game. They were in awe as they watched batting practice and then the game. The thing that I remember were the four or five days prior to the All-Star Game. The weather was absolutely horrible. It rained and rained, day and night, and everyone was concerned that, even though we had the artificial turf, it wouldn't drain. Club officials already realized that the turf didn't drain as well as they'd hoped. But, they squeegeed it off and ran a Zamboni kind of thing over it, and the grounds crew remarkably got the field and stadium in shape in spite of some terrific odds.

On top of that, the big scoreboard, which was kind of a marvel at the time, had been hit by lightening two or three days prior and I don't think they got that thing fixed until about 45 minutes before the game started. There was a bit of panic about that.

Suddenly, around 4:00 on the afternoon of the game, the clouds miraculously rolled away and it was a gorgeous night. You wouldn't have known that the four or five days and nights prior were just about as bad as you could get.

For me, there are games I remember and games I forget, but a lot of my memories from Kauffman Stadium center around the elements.

For instance, one moment that's vivid is when then-American League President Lee MacPhail presented George Brett with his Silver Bat award at the start of the 1977 season. It was George's first of three batting titles, and he was understandably excited to receive the award. The only problem, of course, was the weather.

Since thunderstorms usually roll in from the northwest, the key at Kauffman Stadium has always been to play the flag in left field. The wind swirls so much inside the bowl that, for whatever reason, the flags in left were the best indicators of how the ball would travel in the field — better than looking at the flags in right. When the wind would shift from the southwest and the flag turned with a vengeance, starched out, you knew something was coming. (I'm using past tense because only time will tell if the new construction unveiled in 2009 will affect the ball differently or not.) As soon as the flags shifted, the late Hank Bauer, who was a great player for the Yankees and then became a scout based in Kansas City, grabbed his notebook and was out of there, blasting up those steps.

This particular game when George was receiving his Silver Bat, you could hear the thunder in the background and see some wicked lightning right outside the stadium. When MacPhail presented George with the Silver Bat, there suddenly was a huge clap of thunder and some impressive lightning in the near distance. After George took the Silver Bat, he stood at home plate, and held the bat as high as he could reach, showing everybody his new award. We were thinking, "Oh, no, we're going to lose the American League President and the league's best hitter with one crack of lightning!" They were both going to fold up like a couple of cheap lawn chairs, completely spoiling the pregame festivities.

Another night that stands out for some horrific reasons was what we've come to know as the Plaza Flood. The rain dumped on Kansas City in the middle of September 1977. It was an incredible season on the field for the Royals, and we had great crowds almost every night. Beginning on the night of September 12, though, the city received about 16 inches of rain, and, as a result, 25 people died.

The Royals had a game that night that ended up getting washed out. Sadly, as I remember, a few of those 25 people who died were coming home from the stadium. One really cool thing happened, though, that night that many people forget.

As great as he was as a player, Amos Otis really hadn't become a fan favorite yet. Until *after* that game. See, A.O. stopped at the Holiday Inn across the street from the stadium to get a quick dinner before heading home. Eight boys, wet and shivering, sat outside the hotel. The boys had been trying to get home, but they got stuck and their parents couldn't pick them up because of the flooding. The hotel manager wouldn't let the boys' parents book a hotel room. They were stuck there. That's when A.O. decided to help. He tried to book a room for the boys, but no luck. So, he drove them to his house.

He fed them, had them call their parents, and then took them home the next day. One of the eight boys, now grown men, told Matt Fulks the story for the book *More Than the Score.*

RICH BROWN: "I was one of the eight kids that was stranded during the flood that hit Kansas City, and was taken home from the stadium by Amos Otis. It was reported in The *Kansas City Times* in an article, "An Otis Unknown to Many." Until that point, many fans had a dislike for A.O. off

Amos Otis combined speed with intelligence to become an excellent base runner.

the field. After this story came out of how he took the eight of us to his Blue Springs apartment and bought us dinner, the public saw another side of him.

"After he couldn't get us rooms at the Holiday Inn, all eight of us piled into his new white Lincoln Continental and he took us to a Jack in the Box on Noland Road. It was raining really hard when we pulled up to the drive-through and A.O. had to holler into the speaker so the people inside could hear him. The woman refused us service because she said A.O. was yelling at her (she did not know it was Amos Otis). So, he did the next best thing — he bought us whatever kind of microwave sandwich we wanted at a 7-11.

"The next day, a couple of the kids got dropped off at their houses and A.O. met the parents. My parents did not get to meet him, because when we got to my neighborhood, the roads were closed, and A.O. warned us that he could not swim. He let me out and I caught a Metro bus the rest of the way home.

"Before the following Saturday's home game, Otis had all of us meet in front of the double glass doors at Royals Stadium, and he took us into the clubhouse prior to the game while he got dressed. It was a cool experience.

"I had read a story in *The Star* a couple of years ago about what happened to the kid that (former Chiefs running back) Joe Delaney rescued, and how he turned out. Unfortunately, that young man did not make good choices with his life. I want to let A.O. know that I graduated college, obtained an M.A., became a public school teacher and have been named to 'Who's Who Among America's Teachers' twice in my career.

"You could say that A.O. and that night in 1977 had a huge, positive impact on my life that I'll never forget as long as I live."

Amos and I almost always got along great. There were times that he was, well, A.O., and he'd post signs on his locker that read, "No interviews tonight." But he was just funny that way. He was also one of the sneaky guys in the clubhouse. He'd play practical jokes on his teammates.

One of Jerry Terrell's favorite stories is a time A.O. got a taste of his own medicine.

JERRY TERRELL: "Amos couldn't stand that I was a little, skinny guy, but I kept telling him that I outweighed him. He'd say I didn't, and we'd go back and forth. Finally, he said, 'Let's go to the scales.' What he didn't know was that (trainer Mickey Cobb) and I cooked up a plan. Mickey had those small circle weights, and he took two 5-pound weights and put them in my back pockets. Amos got on the scale and he was something like 185 pounds. I got on and I was 189. He got so mad. 'There's got to be something wrong with the scale. Somebody's messing with it.' I told him to adjust it however he wanted to. Well, bottom line, each time, no matter what he did, I was 3-5 pounds heavier than Amos. He'd go into (equipment manager) Al Zych's room and start grabbing candy bars, anything else to add weight. This went on for 30 days. Thirty days! It got to a point where I was putting two 10-pound weights in my pockets. After 30 days, he was up to 197 pounds. Mickey convinced me that we needed to tell Amos. So, we got on the scale one more time. Amos weighed 197. Then, I got on...175. He couldn't believe it! Mickey held up the weights and said, 'Are you looking for these, Amos?' That was the longest prank I was ever involved with. To this day, Amos looks at me and asks, 'Got any weights in your pockets?'"

Although specific games don't necessarily stand out, one that's memorable because of something on the field, of sorts, happened in the late 1970s. The Royals still had a great rivalry with the Oakland A's that began when Charles Finley took his club from Kansas City to Oakland, and it continued until the Royals overtook the A's in the American League West standings.

On this particular night, it was a packed, electric house. That attitude changed quickly. In the top of the first inning, Joe Rudi drilled a double into the corner for the A's. And then, whack! And another! Three batters, three absolute blasts. The Royals were better than the A's at this point, so it was somewhat odd that they'd drill a Royals pitcher like that.

After the third batter, Whitey Herzog came out of the dugout, and went up to the home plate umpire and started talking to him. Then, Whitey and the home-plate umpire walked down the third-base line and said something to the third-base umpire.

We were trying to guess on the air what might be the issue, when it hit me. For whatever reason, I said on the air, "Maybe Whitey thinks they're stealing signs." And I went on to say how there could be someone in the bullpen with binoculars, looking into the Royals catcher to see what pitch they're calling, and then someone else could signal to the batter.

As soon as I said that, Whitey and the umpires started walking toward the A's bullpen in left field. The Oakland players let Whitey and the umpires in there — which is pretty incredible, when you think about it. When they walked down the line of chairs, hmmm, there was a towel. Oops! Somebody picked it up and there were the binoculars, which the umpire held up.

Whitey wasn't a paranoid manager, but that was a great call on his part.

There also was a time when a visiting manager thought the Royals were up to no good at Kauffman Stadium. From 1983-96, John Martin, the artist who paints all of the Royals Hall of Fame portraits, designed the annual Royals Yearbook, including taking many of the photos for the book. John, who does remarkable work, always looked for unique pictures to take for the Yearbook.

JOHN MARTIN: "In the early 1980s, I thought it would be unique to take some pictures from the top of the old scoreboard, from the crown. It gave us unusual shots from a great angle, about 10 stories up. There was a spiral staircase that you'd take up there, and then you'd get out on a landing. Above that was the back of the speakers. The first time we went up there, there were some ladders that workers were using to repair the light bulbs in the crown. I decided to climb up the ladder to get an even better view. When we were on the ladders, the music between innings came on and started blaring out of those speakers. It was so loud that I thought the vibration was going to blow us off the scoreboard! I'm surprised we didn't lose our hearing.

"The third time my friend, Harv Gareity, and I went up there to take some pictures, the Chicago White Sox were in town. Tony LaRussa was their manager. Harv was on one side at the bottom of the curve in the crown, and I was on the other side. Of course, we had big telephoto lenses on the cameras. Harv had a portable radio and he was listening to Denny and Fred. This was around the middle of the game, and Harv told me, 'They're asking us to get down.' I asked him who. 'The umpires. Denny and Fred are talking about it on the radio.' Evidently, LaRussa spotted us and told catcher Carlton Fisk to say something to the umpires. LaRussa thought we were up there stealing their signals. If we didn't have that radio up there, we wouldn't have known they'd even stopped the game because of us. From that angle, it just looked like the umpires were signaling to the outfield. Of course, we got down, but we ended up getting some television coverage from it. That was quite an experience."

One manager who certainly was paranoid of the Royals and any other team facing his was Billy Martin. Of course, there was the "Pine Tar Game" and all of the times Billy would stop a game to point out a missed call — at least in his eyes — to the umpires. But, I think some of that paranoia ran over to Billy's players.

GEORGE TOMA: "Catfish Hunter was one of my greatest friends. When he was with the Kansas City A's, he was a bonus player. At that time, you had to spend one year on the roster. That fall, he went hunting with his brother and his brother shot him in the leg. So Charlie Finley sent Catfish up to the Mayo Clinic to get the pellets out. But Charlie didn't want him hanging around the experienced ballplayers – you can guess why – so he had Catfish hang around with the grounds crew, and we got close. Then when he went to Oakland and later the Yankees, he couldn't win in Kansas City. (Yankees owner) George Steinbrenner got so mad that he ordered the league to have the umpires watch us the day Catfish was going to pitch. We never did anything to the mound or anything like that. He'd come in, put a chew in his mouth, put his sweatshirt on, and come talk to the kids. When he'd leave, we'd throw him a putty knife and say, 'Son, you'll need this tonight.' It psyched him out."

Although, with George Toma on the Royals' side, the club had a bit of a home-field advantage. Not just by psyching out an opposing pitcher or with the impeccable way they manicured the field. Well, maybe a little bit with the field.

GEORGE TOMA: "Sometimes we would do things that we'll call 'groundskeeping by deceit.' Mickey Mantle didn't care for (Municipal) because I kept centerfield hard and it was hard on his legs. One of my best buddies and a guy who serves as a coach for the Twins during spring training is Harmon Killebrew, who played with the Royals. I used to keep third base like concrete because Harmon could hit that ball but he was a little slow. (An opposing team's) trainer would tell me, 'You're going to get my third baseman killed down there!" So we'd make it hard to make sure the ball would get through the infield. Groundskeeping by deceit.

"Guys like Steve Busby always wanted a little hole next to the rubber so he could push off. ... In the batter's box, there used to be a special hole for George Brett and a special hole for Amos Otis and for Hal McRae. We did a lot of cheating because we moved the batter's box back about 10 inches. If we got caught, I'd blame it on my son, Chip. Everything went great until the Royals traded Buck Martinez to Milwaukee. The first time they came to town, manager George Bamberger came up to me and said, 'George, I don't want any of that stuff, moving that batter's box.'

"We could do a lot of things. (At Municipal with the A's,) we had a Butternut clock on the left field tower. It had two dots. ... We would send Bobby Hoffman into the scoreboard before the game and then we'd get the other team's signals. If those two dots were on, it was a fastball. If one dot was on, it was a breaking pitch. Or, they could look down the third-base line to Charlie O's (the mule) pen. If the lantern was on, that was a fastball. If the lantern was off, it was a breaking pitch. All of that was just part of the game back then."

Fortunately or unfortunately, that cheating evidently never paid off for the Kansas City A's. They didn't have a winning season in any of their 13 years spent in Kansas City.

One Yankee player got a chance to play one season in Kauffman Stadium as a member of the Royals: Lou Piniella. Sweet Lou was a piece of work. His temperament hasn't changed much. He was a fun guy to be around, but he could be very volatile.

When the Royals started play in 1969, with Lou as their left fielder, they wore the button-down jersey tops. Every once in a while, Lou would get so frustrated when making an out, that he'd throw his bat and helmet and then, when he didn't have anything left, he'd grab his jersey by the collar and pull on it as hard as he could. Of course, all of the buttons would go rocketing off. It's a wonder it didn't put someone's eye out.

Speaking of eyes, we were playing a Saturday afternoon game at Municipal on a sunny, hot day. Lou hit into an inning-ending double play. As expected, he rounded first base after the out, cussing and kicking the dirt and grass to vent his frustration. Shortstop Freddie Patek brought out Lou's glove with his sunglasses inside. Lou impatiently grabbed the glove and sunglasses, and stomped out to left field still thinking about how he had just finished the inning with a double play. He was steaming!

He took his hat and jammed it onto his head, crooked. Then, he took his sunglasses and chucked them into left field, along with his glove. And he kept walking in that direction. Lou got out there, picked up the glasses, put them on his head, and then grabbed his glove. He was still steaming!

The second batter that inning, hit a high fly ball to left field. As Lou was getting ready to field the sun ball, he hadn't realized that when he threw his glasses on the ground, one of the lenses popped out. So when he flipped down the glasses for this fly ball, he was blinded in one eye from the sun. With one lens in and one lens out, Lou started spinning around like a top out there, trying to get an angle on the ball. He just kept spinning out of control. Somehow, though, he ended up making the catch.

As Lou's gone on to a great career as a manager, it's nice to see that his temper hasn't gotten the best of him. OK, well, at least he doesn't have to worry about his sunglasses.

One game-specific story from Kauffman Stadium before moving on. Last chapter I mentioned Kevin Seitzer's defensive lapse in Minnesota. So I don't leave Seitz hanging, one story worth mentioning is the day in August 1987 that he went six-for-six against the Red Sox.

Seitz had been tearing up American League pitching that entire season, which was his rookie year. This particular day against Boston, he became the second player in Royals history to get six hits in a game. And it's a wonder he got up a sixth time.

KEVIN SEITZER: "The part about that story that's most amazing to me is that we were killing them, and we came up in the bottom of the eighth inning, and I was six guys from getting to the plate for my sixth at-bat. There were two outs and a couple guys on base. Lonnie Smith, who was ahead of me, was going to the plate with two outs. He waited for me to get out to the on-deck circle and he said, 'I've never seen anybody get six hits before. You're going to get a chance.' I thought, 'That's a pretty cool statement, but just get up there and hit.' I didn't think anything about it until that sucker got a base hit to left field. I got goose bumps. I walked to the plate thinking, 'This dude's giving me a chance to get another AB (at-bat).' It was amazing. It's like Babe Ruth calling his shot.

"I was facing their closer, and I got a sunball double to right field for my sixth hit. Mike Greenwell, Boston's right fielder, went over for it, lost it in the sun and kind of alligator-armed it. I appreciate him doing that. Really, though, it was just another at-bat. You're excited to get the chance, but I always just tried to do my thing. My college coach taught me to focus and not try to do too much. That's what I did day-in and day-out. It wasn't as if I was going to put an 'S' on my chest, jump out of a phone booth and do something special. It was just another at-bat in the game. Of course, there were games when I went four-for-four and five-for-five, but to get that sixth opportunity in a game was amazing. I still get goose bumps talking about it now."

So do we, Kevin. So do we.

Crosby, Stills, Nash and ... Herk?

Long-time Royals executive Herk Robinson has spent as much time at the stadium as anyone else, probably, including a long stint as the man who oversaw stadium operations.

HERK ROBINSON: "I think Kauffman Stadium is as good as any stadium that's ever been built, which is reinforced when you see this much money being put in to remodel it. ... I know there had been sentiment to put the stadium downtown. It would've been wonderful if people could've guaranteed that downtown Kansas City would be like downtown Cleveland or downtown Baltimore and other similar places that are heaven on earth. I'll say respectfully that if you want to kill the Royals quickly, move the team downtown. When other stadiums went downtown, there was already an established downtown and they became the crown jewel. But to put a stadium in downtown hoping it becomes vibrant is a big risk.

"It speaks well for the stadium when you put, basically, a new shell around the old field. I think it's a testament to the stadium."

Former Royals GM Herk Robinson and I enjoyed a trip to legendary Wrigley Field.

Most long-time Kansas City residents can tell you that the Beatles performed at Municipal Stadium when the A's were playing here. But, did you know that Kauffman Stadium hosted some concerts shortly after it opened? Just ask Herk. He remembers. I don't think he'll ever forget them, actually.

HERK ROBINSON: "We had several rock concerts in the early 1970s that made my hair go gray and go away. You didn't know if the stadium would be standing in three hours. Joe Burke, one of my predecessors as General Manager, was so opposite of a rock concert. He'd be leaving at 5 on a Friday afternoon, and I'd say, 'Joe, you have to stay all weekend for this thing.' He'd just shake his head and say, 'Nope,' and walk out quickly.

"We had eight or 10 that were old-fashioned rock concerts when we didn't know if the stadium would be standing the next morning.

Promoters wanted to put a jazz festival there, but they said it wouldn't start until midnight and then it'd go until 3 or 4 in the morning. I said, 'You have the wrong place, then.' We weren't going to do that. I could write a book about the concerts. Some of them included Crosby, Stills, Nash and Young; Lynyrd Skynyrd; Peter Frampton; and so on. Big names then. We had 40,000 people, just all over the stadium. We had four first-aid rooms and ambulances lined up. People didn't really respect the police, so we couldn't really use them, but one night people got on the horizontal part of the net that used to cover the seats behind home plate. Police took about six guys off the net and took them to jail. The whole place rioted. They came outside the stadium and started pushing the fences down, and someone drove a car through Gate B and into the stadium. We didn't publicize a lot of that. We didn't have to.

"The concerts were very profitable, but finally Mr. Kauffman said we shouldn't do it. They wanted to take over the whole stadium. The wine had to be chilled at the perfect temperature, and then some of them wanted M&Ms of a certain color. It went on and on. Of course, George Toma would get mad because of the field. They were very scary."

Motley Going Back....No Outs to Go....The Royals Have Won the 1985 World Series!

Throughout this book, you'll read a few stories about the Royals during the 1985 season, including the playoffs against Toronto and the World Series against the Cardinals. Since the Royals won the title at home, though, in one of the defining moments for Kauffman Stadium, I want to end with a couple cool stories from Willie Wilson.

Of course, Willie was the Royals centerfielder for many years, including '85. In the seventh and deciding game of the Series, he had an interesting role on big moments in the second inning and the ninth inning.

As most Royals fans remember, Darryl Motley crushed a John Tudor pitch for a home run in the second inning. You might also remember that on the pitch before the homer, he mashed another Tudor pitch that went foul by a few feet. Something Willie told Motley after Willie faced Tudor in the first inning became vital in that at-bat.

WILLIE WILSON: "We'd faced Tudor twice already in the World Series. In his third game against us, he started me off with more fastballs than he had in the other two games. In those games, he was throwing more changeups. He'd go fastball and then double up with his changeup. He just had his pattern. This time, in the first inning, I grounded out to second, on a fastball. He doubled up two fastballs. I said to Mot before he went up there, 'He's doubling up his fastballs. Just keep looking for the fastball.' Mot hit that first fastball foul and broke his bat. And then Tudor threw another one and Mot hit out of the ballpark."

Then, there's Motley catching the final out of the game in the Royals' 11-0 win. That was a ball Willie badly wanted to catch. But not for the reason you might think.

WILLIE WILSON: "Nobody seems to remember this, but we were all on the bench and I thought I heard someone say, 'Whoever catches the last out, everybody pays him 25 bucks.' That's all I heard. As Mot and I were jogging to the outfield for the ninth inning, I'm telling him, 'I'm gonna get this last one.' I wasn't even thinking about the World Series; I was thinking about that 25 bucks from 25 guys. If you look at the film, Mot was standing there (for the final out) and I was running over, calling for the ball. But Mot caught it. I was just so excited, though. All of us were. That's a pretty special moment."

And it remains one of the highlights in Kauffman Stadium's history. It always will be. Over the course of time, this stadium has seen its share of ups and downs.

A fairly recent "up" was 2003, when the Royals got off to a hot start, winning their first nine games and building their record to 16-3 before finishing the season with an 83-79 record, good for third place in the American League Central. That was a season that the club had a legitimate chance at a playoff spot. Joe Randa was one of the keys to that club. He batted .291 with 16 home runs and 72 runs driven in.

JOE RANDA: "When I was coming up in 1995, there was so much history with the Royals as a model franchise. All of us in the minor leagues were very excited and proud to be in this organization. Everybody wanted to be a part of that. When you got into Kauffman Stadium and you saw those (championship) flags, you knew how special it was to be there. Wally Joyner told me on my first day in the big leagues, 'You should be very proud to be wearing that jersey.' He wasn't even here in those glory years, but he knew the history and he felt it as a veteran player.

"People kept telling us about the excitement at Kauffman Stadium during the 1970s and '80s. I didn't really feel that, though, until 2003. So many magical things were happening and people were talking about us in the community. There was a buzz that hadn't been here since the '80s. To come through some of those tough years in the 1990s, and then getting over the hump in 2003 was special. We felt that momentum, which was very cool."

In spite of the bad, because of the good, and hopeful for the future, Kauffman Stadium remains a beautiful place for the club to call home. During an opening home stand in late 1990s, after looking out and seeing the natural grass surface and all of the trees and shrubbery, I said on the air, "When this place opened, it was a stadium; now, with the changes they've made, it's a ballpark." I think with the major renovations before the 2009 season, it's truly a gem again.

Fan's Question: I've always been curious about something. When you guys, the broadcasters and writers, are on a plane with the team, is there an understood line that you don't cross? Is there a "right time" and a "wrong time" to approach the players on the team plane?

Chris Garrett
Leawood, Kansas

Denny: There's no line; you can do whatever. But most people stay to themselves. Guys are usually sleeping, reading, playing cards, eating, watching movies, etc. It's not really a social hour. People just do their own things. Rarely are there eight or 10 guys just shooting the breeze. Everybody has their iPods, DVD players, books and so on these days. For most of them, the time on the plane is their time to unwind and relax.

CHAPTER FOUR
It's Not As Easy As It Looks

Question: How often have you been sitting around with your buddies, talking about a pitching change the Royals manager made during the game, or how a hitter struck out three times in a contest, or a deal the Royals general manager pulled the string on, and someone (perhaps you) blurted out: "Man, even I could do that!"?

Come on, you know you've done it. Maybe not with the Royals and maybe not even in baseball, but we've all questioned some type of move or transaction and decided that we could've done a better job. I've done it. *Every* sports fan has done it.

One thing I've learned by being around a Major League Baseball team for more than 40 years is that oftentimes it's not as easy as it looks. So, before you start thinking you can do a job with the Royals better than someone else, you might want to learn a little more first about some of those jobs.

General Manager

Characteristics and the role: The general manager's job has changed so drastically since I started in 1969, when Cedric Tallis was the Royals general manager. They work hand in hand with the manager — that much has stayed the same. But, in the late '60s and early '70s, the job focused mainly on acquisitions and player personnel.

I don't think Cedric, who was the GM from 1969 until midway through the '74 season, was concerned with tickets and travel and that sort of thing. The job was simpler, more narrowly defined. It wasn't simpler in terms of being an easy job, because it definitely was difficult. But the general manager then had more of a single focus of what was happening on the field.

Today, the job is involved with player personnel, but the general manager also oversees extraneous things. That began to change in the late 1980s and into the '90s. It certainly was changing when Herk Robinson was the Royals general manager from 1990-2000.

HERK ROBINSON: "I think it's a tremendous honor to be a general manager. A great responsibility and a very, very difficult job. It's not like opening 12 doughnut shops knowing they all can be successful. You know in baseball that for every win, there's a loss. There are other clubs that are attempting to do what you are, and some of them are maybe doing it better. When I was doing it, it was a 24-hour, 7-day-a-week job. I remember waking up on the morning before Christmas Eve in 1993 hearing the White Sox got Tim Raines. It ruined my whole Christmas because we didn't get him. So, it's an extremely competitive job in which you're dealing with a lot of different people. Sometimes it moves at the speed of light and at other times it moves extremely slow because you have to play 162 games to determine a winner.

"When I first started out, some of my heroes were guys like Joe Brown, John McHale and Lee MacPhail. I started working in baseball with the Cincinnati Reds under Bill DeWitt Sr., whose son owns the St. Louis Cardinals. They all were businessmen but I don't know if at that time any of the baseball's GMs were former players. A lot of them owned the club, too. It's changed a great deal. Clubs started hiring former scouts because they had been evaluators. Then I think there might've been a period of time when the guys weren't as conscientious of the dollar as they needed to be. Now I think they've gone back to people who are younger. There are a lot of types of general managers.

"It's a terribly responsible job, or at least you feel that it is. You want to satisfy everyone. In my entire time with the Royals when Mr. Kauffman was alive, he was the only one I cared about satisfying. If the people you work for are satisfied, it's good enough to get by. It's a time-less job that's thankless at times. Nobody really cared about what could have been or may have been or what was close. It didn't make a difference. Any way you look at it, the bottom line is winning and losing."

In essence, today's baseball general manager is like a CEO. That club, and all of the people working there, including every department from marketing and ticketing to public relations, are shaped more in the GM's mold. To put it in perspective, when the Royals won their first division championship in 1976, there were 26 people employed in the club's front office. It's approximately three times that many now. Although the general manager remains to be graded solely on trades that he makes — which might be the least glamorous part of a job — the entire job description is more complicated now than it once was.

Before Dayton Moore became the general manager of the Royals in the summer of 2006, John Schuerholz was asked to describe the job of GM.

JOHN SCHUERHOLZ: "Challenging, demanding, invigorating, exhilarating, frustrating. It's very demanding, especially in today's game because each decision we make has such a dramatic and dynamic financial impact on the value of our franchises and the investment our owners have made. Twenty years ago, a general manager's mistake might cost an organization $25,000 or $50,000, and a bad mistake was $100,000. Now you're talking about tens of millions of dollars.

"Times have changed, but that's the way it is. Good, successful companies and industries anywhere understand the impact of change. They become effective at managing change and they make it work for them. Sometimes you have to change approaches and systems, although I don't think you change philosophies."

When John became the general manager of the Royals in 1981, he obviously inherited a very good team. It was a team that had been to the World Series in '80. Then, when Dick Howser became manager, he and John worked well together and showed how a team should look in all facets. John was fairly conservative in his approach, but he had a very good feel for the game and the GM's job. He also was a good negotiator.

I was a little surprised when John left for Atlanta after the 1990 season, but he got a sweetheart of a deal there. The Braves had been so bad for so long that it was a no-lose situation for John because if the club went any direction, it had to be up. Frankly, the Braves became a championship organization because of John. The amazing thing to me is how they've maintained it for so long. From John's first season, the Braves won 14 consecutive division titles. Their streak ended in 2006. There isn't another club today that's had such an incredible championship stretch. It's one thing to get to the top from the bottom, but quite another to stay there.

Herk Robinson took over after John left, and he directed the club through a difficult time. Herk and Mr. K had a great rapport. After Mr. K died, Herk didn't have an owner to report to. He suddenly had a trust of about 10 people involved, which complicated his task. He was the bridge in everything. I think he did an outstanding job given the parameters within which he had to work.

HERK ROBINSON: "When Mr. Kauffman was alive, you knew what he expected and you knew succinctly how to go about the job, balancing the business side and the baseball side. In the latter years of his life, he tried moving the club to somebody who'd keep it in Kansas City and operate it at his expectations. During the transition after Mr. Kauffman passed away, I reported directly to David Glass, who was Chairman of the Board, and Mike Herman, who was President, and they had a board of directors. Our goals were relatively simple. Financially, we had to be careful not to incur much debt. We wanted to keep the club competitive. It was difficult enough to market the club because it was small market — not arguably a small market, but arguably maybe *the* smallest market. That in itself, I think they could've found plenty of buyers if the club could've been moved to some of the locations, perhaps, that were available at that time. But, that was not going to happen under any conditions.

"It was difficult to get employees to come to work on a long-term basis because change was inevitable. When the club was purchased, you knew there'd be changes. Anybody who came in, even players to a degree, who felt there wasn't a driving force financially to produce a winning ballclub, hindered things somewhat. Operating the club at that time was tricky. We operated under Mr. Kauffman's philosophy unless David Glass or Mike Herman felt otherwise."

In the summer of 2006, after Allard Baird served as general manager, Dayton Moore came to Kansas City from Atlanta, where he worked under John Schuerholz. Obviously, that was a great training ground.

One thing we all learned about Dayton when he first became the club's general manager is his long-time appreciation of the Royals. He was born in Wichita, his dad had grown up in Wichita and his mom grew up in Coldwater, Kansas. She had relatives there, so the Moore family would load up the car and head there every summer, regardless of where they lived.

DAYTON MOORE: "The Royals are the first team that I fell in love with growing up. ... I always followed the Royals. I developed an affection for the Royals through my grandmother, who loved the Kansas City Royals. Her dad and uncles all were baseball players in the local sandlots. So I evoked an affinity for the Royals.

"Then, Dave Larson, a teammate at Garden City Community College, and I watched (Game Seven of the 1985 World Series) from I-70. We were coming from Illinois, where we had both gone to high school, returning to Garden City, and we thought we'd stop and try to buy tickets. We found out fast that we couldn't afford them. And there were a lot of people up there on the hill, so we decided to watch up there. The only thing we couldn't see was Lonnie Smith in left field. But we could feel the energy of the crowd. There were a couple guys up there from Omaha, and they had one of those small battery-operated TVs, and a grill. It was fun."

I don't really know Dayton that well yet. But I will say that he definitely has a plan for turning the Royals back into a winning organization. My perception is that he's going to stay with his plan. I don't think he'll panic and dump it. That's solid. I think he has the ability to be an excellent general manager. Herk mentioned how the job of general manager entails dealing with a lot of different people. Dayton is very good at that. He fits that term of "people person" very well.

DAYTON MOORE: "I hope (my biggest strength) is listening to people. Hiring good people and then letting them do their jobs. Ultimately, the job is listening to people, motivating people, encouraging people, and doing everything I can in my power to make them better. That's what effective leaders do. Effective leaders get out of the way and let leaders lead. That's what I've always tried to do in positions that I've had."

Before leaving the topic of general managers, there's one man who wasn't a general manager with the Royals, but he worked closely with GMs Cedric Tallis and Joe Burke, while helping groom John and Herk: Lou Gorman. After leaving Kansas City, he eventually became a general manager for Boston and Seattle. The main reason I want to include Lou is for what became known around the front office as "Gormanisms." Lou would get so excited sometimes when talking, that his words didn't exactly come out the way he intended. It became so funny, that John and Herk wrote these malapropisms (Gormanisms) and kept them hidden deep inside their desks.

For instance, at the end of one spring training, the powers that be were considering the fate of various players, as is the case at the end of every spring training. Lou had a difficult time deciding what to do with a kid named Joel Bishop. Lou said, "We were faced face to face with the face of Joel Bishop." Huh?

Here are a few of my favorite Gormanisms:

- "We're going to have to start eating the meal money." (Well, money is made of trees, I guess.)
- "That car burns gas like it's eating peanuts." (Is that a good thing these days?)
- "I'll keep my ears posted." (Sounds painful.)
- "I vaguely and vividly remember in my own mind." (I think I remember having days like that.)
- "We're glad to have you with you." (I'm guessing that guy was, too.)
- "He looked like he threw real good just listening on the radio." (Talk about a word picture.)
- "It has real high ceilings covered with paintings and tapestries." (Interesting ceiling.)

- "The toe nail on the top toe is growing into the nail." (Again, sounds painful.)

Manager

Characteristics and the role: The manager's job, also, has changed over time because the players' attitudes have changed. The big difference having talked to people around baseball for a long time is that, at one time, the manager was the boss. He was in charge. Now it seems, with the big salaries and players moving around, the manager doesn't have the hammer he once had. His only hammer now is how much someone's going to play. Facets of the job would include how you run the game and how you use your players. Do you put your players in the best position to succeed? Do you expect a player to do something he can't do? How do you use your bullpen? Talk about being involved with every pitch, compound that for the manager. The coaching staff is valuable now because of that. He deals mostly with the bench coach and the pitching coach.

The manager and his bench coach really have to work in concert. He has to know him and trust him. The bench coach is not in a position to second-guess the manager. Like a manager, he has to think ahead and suggest things. He's trying to leave no stone unturned, which is invaluable to the manager. As far as the pitching coach, he might say to the manager, so and so looks like he's getting tired, should we get somebody up?

Then there are the off-the-field issues for the manager. How do you deal with players as men? And, you have to deal with the media and appearance requests. It's all about trying to keep the general manager happy while keeping the players happy and productive.

Throughout the history of the Royals, we've had guys who were both extremes. Joe Gordon, the club's first manager, and Bob Lemon, for instance, were well-liked managers. Charlie Metro, the man between Joe and Lem, was a task master and a little too stern for a young team. Then there was Jack McKeon, the first Royals manager with a pre-game radio show. He was great for the young guys, but didn't relate too well with the veterans.

Maybe the two best managers in terms of working with players that the Royals have had were Whitey Herzog and Dick Howser.

Whitey, who succeeded McKeon, infused a great spirit and confidence into the team that they were lacking. He was a great manager for young guys, which is what the club had a lot of with guys like Frank White, George Brett, Dennis Leonard and Steve Busby. Whitey had that uncanny ability of knowing which guys needed a swift kick and which ones needed a pat on the back. (And which ones needed both.)

I had suspicions that something was wrong with Dick Howser before he was diagnosed with cancer.

Whitey just knew what to tell players. He was a very smart manager — he never was out-managed. He had a great sense of timing on offense, pitching changes, everything. He is a baseball guy in every sense of the word.

WILLIE WILSON: "You need a manager who will let you try things on the field. One thing about Whitey Herzog that I'm grateful for is that he would let us play innings one through seven. 'Go play the game, boys. Go do what you want to and if it's messed up, I'm taking over after the seventh.' We put on our own hit-and-runs and our own steals. If I was on first base and tapped my helmet, the batter knew I was running on the next pitch. Whitey let us play. If the game was close after the seventh he'd tell us he was taking over."

Dick Howser, who came to the Royals after the 1981 strike, was similar to Whitey. When he first got here, he had a good group of veteran players with which to work. Then, by the time the younger players who would help win the 1985 World Series came up, Dick was established and worked well with young and older players alike. He usually didn't ask guys to do something they couldn't do.

MARK GUBICZA: "Even behind in the first postseason series (in 1985) against Toronto and, of course, against St. Louis, we knew that someone would come up with a key hit or a key pitch in each game. There was no panic, which I think was a direct reflection on Dick Howser and the fact that he was one of those people who deflected all the criticism and nerves onto himself and absorbed it. He'd always tell us, 'Don't worry about it. Piss on it. We'll get this thing done.' That was his famous line and the only speech he gave pretty much religiously whenever he took the time to make a speech. We knew he was backing us. And we knew that he put people in places to give them a chance to be successful. When you're a manager and you throw one kid who's 19, one who's 21 and one who's 22 in a rotation, you've gotta have a lot of guts. And then you had a guy who was just a throw-in in a trade with Cincinnati, Charlie Leibrandt. The anchor of the staff was Bud Black, who was pretty young and inexperienced himself.

"As a kid coming up, we had respect and it was 'Mr. Howser' or whatever, but you felt on an even playing field with him. He wasn't a critical guy. If you threw a bad pitch or took a bad swing, he had the same expression in the dugout. You see that same type of thing in someone like Joe Torre. There never panic on (Howser's) face, which is why he was so good."

The toughest thing I've dealt with as a broadcaster was Dick's battle with cancer, a battle he lost eventually. Through the manager's show, I might have been one of the first ones to realize there was something wrong. Dick was very cautious about what he'd say during the pregame show because he didn't want to give too much away. Around the middle of June in 1986, we would be taping the show and he would not recall something that happened the night before, or he would mix up names. That was odd because he was a sharp thinker. He also looked tired.

As the 1986 All-Star break got closer, the show became increasingly difficult. Then, during the All-Star break, doctors discovered the brain tumor.

Beating brain cancer in the 1980s was nearly impossible. So, most people assumed the odds were stacked against Dick. But the Royals didn't hire a manager full-time. They wanted to leave him with some hope. It was such a difficult time for everyone that, even though there might've been some good managers available, the Royals did the right thing for Dick.

After Dick passed away on June 17, 1987, the Royals began going through a tough stretch for the organization. Several capable managers led the club on the field including former players John Wathan and Hal McRae. That also was just a few years before John Schuerholz left for Atlanta and Ewing Kauffman passed away.

By the time you read this book, at least one or two managers might've manned the Royals. That's the nature of this business. But I think with owner David Glass, general manager Dayton Moore and manager Trey Hillman, the club is headed in the right direction.

Starting Pitcher

Characteristics and the role: Because pitching is so important to winning, especially for a Major League franchise, I developed a profile of a winning starting pitcher. Here are a few of the top characteristics of the guy who's going to get the ball every four or five days. He needs to be ultra competitive without fear. He needs to be emotionally tough. He needs to be smart in a baseball and pitching sense. And he needs to be confident, maybe even a bit arrogant.

The Royals have had so many great starting pitchers, but four who have exemplified those qualities are Paul Splittorff, Dennis Leonard, Mark Gubicza and Zack Greinke.

Splittorff, the first player the Royals ever signed and the first to pitch for the organization (in a minor-league game in 1968), worked hard and was very consistent. He wasn't afraid to challenge hitters and he threw strikes in the process. He had good stuff as a pitcher, but not great stuff. The biggest advantage Split took to the mound each outing — and he started a club-best 392 in his career — was his competitiveness and intelligence.

Leonard, who was the ultimate workhorse for the Royals, got into a mini-war within himself with each hitter. He'd fight you on every pitch. Every time he went to the mound, he had the mindset that he was going to throw for nine innings and come away with a win. And he did those things nearly as well as any pitcher the Royals have had. Think about this: Leo threw 103 complete games, collected 23 shutouts (both firsts in club history), and finished with 144 career wins (second). He also holds three of the top five spots for innings pitched in a season, including the top two with 294 2/3 and 292 2/3 innings, respectively.

Like Leo, Gubicza was a fierce competitor. A right-handed pitcher, he was nasty against right-handed hitters. There wasn't anything smooth or pretty about his delivery, but Gubie endured for a long time before any arm issues. He had a "screw you" mindset like Steve Busby, which is good to have because it tends to put hitters on their heels. As a starting pitcher, you have to make the hitter understand that you know you're in charge. Gubie was very good at portraying that as a pitcher.

BRET SABERHAGEN: "(Gubicza) didn't like to lose. Not that anybody else did, but he took it to an extreme. He was going to pick fights, scream, whatever, to win a ballgame. I can remember us rooming together on the road and his friends coming in from Philly. They were just a bunch of wild and crazy guys that would stir it up in a heartbeat. I remember them coming in and throwing blankets over a couple guys and giving them the 'blanket treatment.' He told the guys that I was off limits, which was great because I was about 165 pounds at the time."

GEORGE BRETT: "If you made an error behind him — you threw one away or the ball went between your legs or a ball went around your glove — you'd get the old Mark Gubicza stare. Sabes (Saberhagen) would turn around and laugh at you, Buddy Black would laugh at you, Charlie Leibrandt would get ticked, but he was a completely different animal than Gubicza. And Danny Jackson would kill you if you made a mistake behind him. Gubie and Danny Jackson were probably two of the hardest guys to play behind because they were so intense that you didn't want to screw up."

Ahhh, the "old Mark Gubicza stare." *Sports Illustrated* had an article about hockey's Mark Messier in the mid-1990s, and it talked about his "stare" and intensity. That was Gubie. It was a look that he gave when he came into the clubhouse on pitching days and carried with him until he was done for the day.

We got along great. Gubie was a huge Philadelphia Flyers fan. I used to tell him that whoever was beating the Flyers was my favorite team. We had a lot of fun with that.

Greinke was cut from a little different mold than other pitchers. Most starting pitchers are starting pitchers. Period. In Zack's mind, he's a baseball player, not just a pitcher. That's different than a Dennis Leonard, Paul Splittorff or Mark Gubicza. Zack enjoys all aspects of the game — fielding, running the bases, hitting. He'd be a tremendous force as a hitter if the American League didn't have the designated hitter. If the pitchers were allowed to hit in the A.L., he would think of himself as a baseball player even more.

He's similar to former Kansas City A's pitcher Lew Krausse. Less than two weeks after his high school graduation in 1961, Lew, one of baseball's first "bonus babies," was starting for the A's. In his debut, he threw a three-hit shutout at Municipal Stadium against the Los Angeles Angels. (Incidentally, the manager for the A's at that time was the man who'd become the first manager in Royals history, Joe Gordon. Just a few days after Krausse's incredible performance, A's owner Charles Finley fired Gordon. He was replaced by a man who made

Profile of a Winning Major League Starting Pitcher

Starting pitching is vitally important in the success of a Major League team. In fact, find me one league champion in the past decade that didn't have good starting pitching. So, a few years ago I developed this profile based on things I've learned during my broadcasting career of watching some of the best (and some of the worst) starting pitchers in baseball.

- Ultra competitive — no fear
- Mentally tough, emotionally stable
- Smart — knows how to pitch — good pitching I.Q.
- Confident, a bit arrogant
- Capable of a strikeout
- Economizes pitches — works quickly, keeps defense involved
- Capable of pitching around errors (physical and mental) — his own and/or his teammates'
- Capable of adjusting — to his stuff, to the hitters, to the game situation — inning to inning, game to game
- Tempo — establishes a good, quick tempo right away. Forces hitters to adjust to his tempo.
- Sets a good example for young players — on and off the field. Gives solid advice if asked.
- Demeanor on the mound should reflect confidence and poise — must give the impression to the opponent that you are "in charge," that you have confidence in your stuff and in your command, and that you are eager to pitch
- Be able to consistently hit the catcher's target with two pitches — preferably three — in each appearance
- Pitches with quick tempo — it upsets a hitter's timing — most hitters don't like to be rushed. Slow tempo also cuts down the range of defenders.
- You can't pitch angry on the Major League level — you over-throw, and lose movement and command
- For a pitcher there's usually one inning that digs deep into the gas tank

Kansas City his home for 40 years, the great Hank Bauer, who was also a player on that team. Want another tidbit? The shortstop on that club and the man who won the American League Rookie of the Year award that season was Dick Howser.) On the night of Krausse's pitching debut, besides what he did on the mound, he went 2-for-3 at the plate.

So, Krausse has said that he went to the stadium the next night *expecting* to be in the lineup. Perhaps as an outfielder. Remember, he was 10 days or so removed from high school, where that type of schedule is normal. But, you can say Krausse was a baseball player, not just a pitcher.

For a player to be good at his position, it's important to enjoy all elements of the game. Baseball players want to play; not just sit and watch. I think that's where Zack is in his career. As a starting pitcher, he enjoys all aspects of the game, but he probably gets a little bored a few days after his start.

Closer

Characteristics and the role: The role of closer is just as much mental as it is physical. If you were being asked to come in and protect a lead 80 times in a season, then it's physical. But it's more mental because you have to accept the pressure. The game's going to be won or lost on your performance. Everyone's counting on you to get the final three outs of the game. For the Royals, that has meant Jeff Montgomery more often than any other closer. Monty ended his career with 304 saves.

JEFF MONTGOMERY: "Being a starting pitcher versus being a relieving pitcher is very different. Even as a reliever it's different because the way you pitch in the fifth, sixth or seventh inning is going to be different than the way you pitch in the eighth and ninth inning. Please don't let anyone ever tell you that pitching the ninth inning is easier than pitching the sixth or seventh inning. I've tried both and it's not. It's always interesting, when I'd be getting mentally ready to go into a game in the eighth or ninth inning, I'm thinking about what guys might be coming up to bat. And I look over at who's sitting on the bench in the other dugout and it might be someone like Harold Baines, who's licking his chops over there. The closer you get to the end of a game, the more weapons an opponent's going to throw at you. I hated when we started a left-handed pitcher, because I knew their very best left-handed hitters weren't starting that day and that meant that a hitter like a George Brett, who oftentimes wouldn't start against a Randy

Johnson, was ready to go. The closer you get to the end, the more you're going to see those weapons.

"That's part of the reason those last three outs are so tough. But I think it's shown to be pretty true to people who watch a lot of baseball. We were playing in Cleveland one year and I had an injury of some type and I was on the shelf for a day or two. We had a left-handed reliever named Billy Brewer. He was throwing the ball really well. Billy and Rusty Meacham had been working together, left hander and right hander, as my set-up guys. They were doing a remarkable job. For some reason, I was on the shelf for this particular game. I was sitting in the bullpen with them, talking them through situations. Cleveland, in their stadium, had a remarkable knack of coming from behind and winning ballgames. Albert Belle made the last out of the game, hitting the ball as far as he could hit it without it leaving the ballpark. Billy Brewer got the save. We were in the clubhouse afterwards, high-fiving each other. Billy said, 'Man, you can have that job back. I don't want any part of that; it's too much.'"

The older guys have been able to compartmentalize a little better and focus only on the task at hand instead of what might've happened in a previous outing. Human emotion has to be figured in, along with confidence, for a closer. That might be the most fragile emotion for an athlete because it's built on not only what you've done in the past but what you've done most recently. If you're fragile mentally, you can't be a closer. That's probably the one element of the closer that's most important.

JEFF MONTGOMERY: "The biggest asset of a closer is a short memory because regardless of how great things are going, you're going to hit a bump occasionally. But to be able to get back on the hot side of things, you have to forget yesterday. If you're doing well, you don't need anything to boost you that day. If you're going bad, you sure don't need anything to bring you down. That's why I think the short memory is good. You have to go out day after day and pitch to your strengths. Forget the scouting reports. You have to pitch to your strengths. The most important part of that is understanding the situation in the game. Who's on their bench? What's our lead? Then, pitch to the situation with your strengths and get the most out of what you have."

One of the Royals' early closers, Doug Bird, could do it all. I think he was competitive but it didn't show like it did with Leo or Gubie. He was a good competitor in whatever role he was asked. Like a Mark Teahen, Bird never had a definitive role. If a pitcher could do it, Birdie was asked to do it. He was in every pitching slot for the Royals. I don't think it was that great for him because he never really settled into what was the best situation for him. The best thing for Birdie, though, was that he had a devil-may-care personality, which was good for him.

One of the Royals' early closers, Doug Bird (right) could do it all. And he filled out a uniform a little better than I did too.

DOUG BIRD: "I liked the short relief because I got more games. Starting, you sit around for four days, even though I was more of a starter when I came up after being short relief. Whitey (Herzog) tried everything. He wasn't afraid to experiment.

"Whitey would fine me $100 every time I threw an 0-2 strike. I didn't believe in wasting pitches. I got a batter 0-2 in Anaheim and he got a base hit on the next pitch. So, here comes Whitey. And he was all over me. I finished the inning. The next inning, Whitey got thrown out of the game. I went back out to pitch and sure enough the first hitter I faced I got ahead 0-2. I threw the next ball up in the radio booth, almost hitting Denny. I could hear Whitey in the runway screaming at me but he couldn't come out because he had been ejected from the game."

In 1978, the Royals got the consistent closer we'd needed throughout the mid-1970s, when Dan Quisenberry came up. I really liked Quiz. He was a little quirky, but confident. Not to the point of cocky, but he knew he could get batters out. He wasn't dominating in the Goose Gossage or Trevor Hoffman kind of way, but hitters couldn't handle his submarine delivery. Besides being such a good person, he had the perfect personality for a closer.

JOHN WATHAN: "We used to sit together in the bullpen. His routine in the bullpen was to do the crossword puzzle early in the game. All of us in the bullpen would try to guess the attendance at home games. So, Quiz and I would sneak back into George Toma's office about the 5th inning and call to find out what the attendance was. We would 'guess' close enough that we won all the time. Nobody could figure out how we did that. Then, he would start to get serious about the 6th inning, and be ready to pitch."

It's funny, but after struggling to get a solid closer through the winning 1970s, the Royals went from Quiz almost right into another oddly consistent closer in Jeff Montgomery, whom they acquired from Cincinnati in exchange for Van Snider.

Monty isn't a big, intimidating guy and wasn't some great closer when he came to Kansas City. The Reds didn't really use him as the closer, and for his first couple of years here, the Royals didn't, either. In 1988, Steve Farr got most of the closer's duty. Farr had been setting up Quiz and he talked to the coaches about how it was his turn to close some games.

What Monty had, though, is something most good closers don't have: four pitches. Closers typically have two pitches. That alone made Montgomery unique. His size — about 5-11 and 180 pounds — made him unique. Put him next to Goose Gossage and they'd look like father and son. But, again, he had four solid pitches and he'd use them regardless of the count or situation.

I had the feeling Monty, when he came out of the bullpen, knew what pitches felt good that night. Even when he got to the mound I think he was sorting through his pitches and deciding what was working. He and the catcher, usually Mike Macfarlane, adjusted beautifully. He had a feel for what the hitter was trying to do. Sparky Lyle could come out of the bullpen and throw nothing but sliders. Mariano Rivera comes in and you're looking for a cut fastball. Different types of closers. Monty certainly was unique.

In 2008, Joakim Soria burst onto the scene with a similar mentality and pitch workability as Montgomery. He was a Rule 5 draft pick for the Royals and mainly pitched as a starter throughout his career. Still, in 2008, he got 42 saves for the Royals. No reliever had even reached 30 saves since Monty's 36 a decade earlier. Soria seems to have a great feel for pitching and he's very smart. So, any adjustments he needs to make as the hitters adjust to him, I think he'll be able to pull it off.

JEFF MONTGOMERY: "One of the biggest keys for someone like Joakim Soria, similar to myself, is you have to get away from the mindset of everyone saying you have to do this or you have to do that. You're not the typical guy. You're trying to get possibly the three toughest outs of the game. Just because the book says you should do it this way, you can't get away from your game. An example for me, if I'd sit in the bullpen for a week without pitching and they'd put me in a blow-out game, the mindset is fastball, fastball, fastball. I'd find myself getting into trouble in those situations because I'd get away from my game. I wouldn't pitch to my strengths. The best thing for me to do in a close game or a blowout was to show all four of my pitches early in my appearance. Once the hitter knows you're going to throw four pitches, it makes every one a more effective pitch.

"I had to do that. I remember a game in Fenway when I was pitching against Mo Vaughn. It was full count, bases loaded, two outs and a one-run game. Mike Macfarlane was catching and he put down a changeup. Of my four pitches, the changeup was the one I had the least command of. That would've been the fourth pitch in my mind that I would've thrown at that time. But when Mac put down the sign, I thought, 'You know, that's the right pitch.' I actually threw a 3-2 changeup with the bases loaded, and Mo Vaughn was so out in front of that that when he swung, he threw his bat over the first-base dugout. The game was over. I threw it and executed it and it was effective. That's an example of having the ability and the confidence that you can throw any pitch at any time."

Every Day Player

Characteristics and the role: Charley Lau told me one time that to play at the big-league level nearly every day, 150-155 games, you have to be strong, both mentally and physically. Sometimes you don't feel 100 percent and want to take the day off. But you have to be consistent. You have to keep playing. It's a similar idea to running a marathon. When you get late in the run, you're hurting. But pretty much every person around you is hurting, too. You just have to keep pushing.

The most demanding of the eight positions is catcher. It's both physically and mentally more demanding because you're involved with every single pitch. Second most demanding would be the middle infield, second and short because they have to know what's going on with every pitch. To a slightly lesser degree are the corner infielders. Then, to take nothing away from the outfielders, they'd be the last three in terms of physical and mental demand on a game-by-game basis because they're sort of on their own island out there. It's a little more relaxing. The outfielders are a unit. Shoot, it's as much of a drain as a broadcaster because you're in such deep concentration for three hours.

One of the early dependable players for the Royals was third baseman Paul Schaal, whom the Royals picked in the 1968 Expansion Draft from the then-California Angels.

PAUL SCHAAL: "From my career, I'm most proud of the fact that my teammates could count on me to play every day. I wasn't a leader, but you could count on me being in the lineup every day. Bob Lemon, when he managed here, said he'd write my name down first because he knew I'd be in the lineup."

To back up that story, Paul played in 161 games in 1971, Lem's first full season with the Royals. The interesting thing about all of that is that Paul got hit in the head by a pitch in '68 and had all sorts of dizziness issues for about six months, along with double-vision, hearing loss, and so on. In fact, on pop ups to the left side of the infield, Paul would hope and count on shortstop Freddie Patek to call him off and catch a lot of those.

PAUL SCHAAL: "I tried to hide that fact during spring training, so I'd go away from the coaches to play catch. I feel I was a good defensive third baseman with the Angels, but I lost that ability because I couldn't focus on the balls. I saw two coming at me. If I dove after a ball, there was a fear there that I'd get more dizziness. So, I decided that if I was going to stay in the big leagues, I'd have to be a better hitter."

In April 1974, the Royals traded Paul back to the Angels for Richie Scheinblum. By that time, the club knew it had its next third baseman, some young kid, who would eventually wear number 5.

PAUL SCHAAL: "I had a very good year in '71 (150 hits, 11 homers, 63 RBIs and a .274 batting average). I went to spring training in '72 knowing the job at third base was mine. That's about the time, though, that I started hearing about this kid named George Brett. I met him for the first time during spring training. He came up to me and said, 'Mr. Schaal, do you mind if I take some ground balls with you?' That was fine but I wasn't ready to give up my job just yet. I've laughed since then that it took a Hall of Famer to take my job from me."

Frank White, one of the best ever to play second base in the history of the game, was both physically and emotionally strong and competitive, night after night. Part of this component is the ability for pitchers to throw strikes and let the hitters put the ball in play. When a pitcher is walking hitters or even going 3-and-2 throughout a game, fielders lose concentration. Frank had such great concentration every night that he'd have to wind down in the clubhouse for a little while before going home.

You always think of Frank, first and foremost, defensively. He came up through the Royals organization as a shortstop, but he made the conversion to second base. He had all the attributes of a great infielder — great hands, quickness, good reflexes, great leaping ability, solid arm, and athleticism. Plus he had sound fundamentals to go with those physical attributes. He was the perfect second baseman because he would make the spectacular plays, but more importantly, he made the routine plays.

Even the routine plays could look incredible with Frank at second. There was one game in Boston when all of Frank's attributes came together and made a routine play look pretty cool.

WILLIE WILSON: "There was a double-play ball and George (Brett) or U.L. (Washington) threw the ball to Frank at second base. Big Jim Rice came barreling into the base and took Frank out. Frank was mad and I think the play hurt his leg a little. A couple innings later, there was the same situation. Frank gets to the bag really quick, he gets the ball, and he threw the ball straight down toward Jim Rice on the ground. The ball hits the ground right next to Jim Rice, who was sliding. Frank threw the ball so hard that it took one bounce and flew to first base in time to get the double play. That's how hard he threw that ball. For the rest of the game, the Red Sox were sliding about 2-3 feet short of second base."

Frank was a very steady player. He played hard. He was durable — he played every game. Then, year to year, he improved offensively. By the time he was in his late 20s, he was a viable offensive force. He achieved what he achieved through hard work and applying himself to the everydayness of Major League Baseball. For all of those reasons he was one of the best second basemen ever, even to a former opponent, such as Tony Muser, who spent most of his career with the Chicago White Sox and Baltimore.

TONY MUSER: "On double plays, I really think players went in harder on Frank than they did anyone else, even moreso back then than they do now because of the style of baseball the Royals played. If you let yourself hang out there on defense, George Brett would get you. Hal McRae would get you. The whole team took on that mentality of 'get you.' When you're gotten, you want to get back, so it was reciprocated. Frank was smart enough and quick enough and tough enough to handle that reciprocation. You know, the headhunter on a hockey team was told he could get anyone except Wayne Gretzky. With Frank it wasn't that way. We were trying to reciprocate and go in hard on him. He was strong enough, smart enough, tough enough that you couldn't get him at second base. And a lot of people tried.

"Frank played at a high level on a consistent basis, so people didn't realize how good he was. He showed up for every single pitch that came off that rubber. If they threw 131 pitches in a game, Frank was there mentally and physically for all 131, not 128, not 130. 131. If they're honest, not many players today can say that they were there for every single pitch in a game. To me, the level at which Frank produced every day, made him a Hall of Fame player."

Another consistent every day player was Joe Randa, who could do most anything, offensively or defensively. There weren't many nicks in his game. He didn't have great speed, but he had excellent quickness and reflexes, and he worked hard. The one thing a manager likes is consistency and that he knows what to expect. Joe gave his managers that. He could be penciled in for 150 games or so a season, and you could count on about a dozen home runs and a batting average not much below .300.

JOE RANDA: "Physically, it takes preparation with your body to be a good every day player. You have to make sure you do your work in the weight room, eat right, and get your rest. You have to take care of yourself every day during the season. The mental side, though, is what I think makes or breaks an every day player. All the guys at this level have the physical tools, but they struggle sometimes to figure out the mental part. Failure in baseball is like no other sport. Being able to deal with that and learn with that is what sets you apart. It took me three or four years when I reached the big leagues to believe in myself and deal with the mental side of failure. Once I figured those things out, the game became more fun. It really helped me as a player.

"The guys who don't dwell on those failures are the ones who have a better chance of being successful. If you worry about an error that you made in the field during the first inning, you'll probably make another one in the sixth inning or maybe even the ninth inning. What sets you apart is being able to put those behind you. The one player who really stands out to me is Derek Jeter. He plays in one of the toughest environments, New York, but he can stay focused and not let things distract him. That's something you have to learn as a player. I was lucky coming up because the Royals still had a veteran team at the Major League level with guys like Greg Gagne, Wally Joyner and Gary Gaetti, who could help teach us those things."

It's interesting that Joe mentioned Jeter. It reminds me of a feature article about John Buck that I read in the Royals *Gameday* magazine in 2007. In a story Buck told, he was catching in a game against the Yankees. The bases were loaded and there were two outs, late in a close contest. Jeter was at the plate, and he kept fouling off pitches. He was doing whatever he could to make contact and keep the at-bat going until he got his pitch.

As Buck said, "After fouling off a few, (Jeter) looked down at me and winked as he was blowing a bubble. I could only think, 'Oh, my gosh, look how relaxed he is.' But he plays (the scenario) through his mind, he knows what he's looking for and he knows what he's capable of. He's relaxed because of that."

Around 2006, the Royals started bringing some of their former guys to Arizona to work with the young players. Joe was one of the alums there in uniform. To have some fun during the broadcast, I took a wireless microphone to the dugout. We were going to do the entire ninth inning together. As luck would have it, the top half of the inning lasted about 45 minutes and the bottom of the ninth lasted 35 minutes. We witnessed some of the worst stuff on the field. Guys were running into each other and falling over. It was uglier than sin, just awful. But we laughed our way through it, talking about everything, including what we got for Christmas. (I'm sure Ryan Lefebvre was dying of laughter in the booth.) Joe was dogged just like he was as a player.

One recent guy who looks like he could become a solid every day player is outfielder David DeJesus. He's built solid, but injuries have held him back a little more than he'd like. To be an every day player, you have to be both strong and lucky. Dave isn't always lucky, but he is a really, really good outfielder. He's made some excellent plays. He's a good guy to have on the team because he plays hard and he's normally upbeat. You need someone like that on a club.

Hitter

Characteristics and the role: One of the greatest conversations (I would love to have a tape of it) I've ever heard in my life was in spring training in 1969 — my first and the Royals' first —when Joe Gordon and Ted Williams were behind the batting cage debating their opposing views of hitting. Joe Gordon's theory was hit down on the ball, while Ted Williams' theory was a sweeping upward type of stroke. The arguing back and forth, the pros and cons of those styles, was absolutely scintillating. It was as compelling a conversation as I've ever heard in my life. It went on for about 20 minutes. It was unbelievable. I wish I had had a tape or a note pad or anything. Heck, even a good memory.

But listening to that conversation made me realize that to be a solid Major League hitter, you have to have the obvious attributes of quick hands and great hand-eye coordination, along with some God-given ability and a little luck.

Much like thinking about Frank White when you hear the words "Royals" and "defense," the first name that pops into most fans' minds when they hear "Royals" and "offense" is George Brett.

Early in my career, the original "voice" of the Royals, Bud Blattner, stressed to me the importance of being my own announcer. I shouldn't imitate him or Jack Buck or Harry Caray or whoever. Bud stressed that otherwise, all I was doing was becoming a bad imitation of the broadcaster I was trying to sound like. I think about that when I think about George's rise in baseball. When he first came up, he held his bat high above his head and had just a goofy stance. He was a bad imitation of one of his childhood heroes, Carl Yastrzemski. When it came to George's swing, he had more holes than a tennis racket. He quickly realized that wasn't going to work for him against Major League pitchers. But George had two things working for him: a great work ethic and Charley Lau.

Right before the All-Star break in 1974, with a return trip to Omaha certainly in his future if George continued hitting sub-.200, Lau, the Royals hitting coach/guru at the time, asked George if he was ready to go to work on his swing. Of course, George was. So, pretty much every afternoon at 3, George headed to the stadium for mandatory work on his swing.

GEORGE BRETT: "When I first started working with Charley Lau in 1974, the most important fundamental, which was probably the hardest for me to pick up — and probably the most influential thing he ever taught me once I picked it up — was extension through the ball and having a weight shift. Before, up until that time, I never really had a weight shift. When you're 8 years old and you start playing baseball in a competitive league, all of a sudden you're 21 years old and he's telling you that you've been doing this all wrong for 13 years, it's tough to break that habit. ... It was hard for me to go ask at first but through continuous hours of batting practice, it worked."

Somehow, Charley, who wasn't more than an average big-league player himself, figured out how to teach hitting. By his nature, he had a wonderful teaching tool: he was incredibly soft-spoken. How does that old commercial go: "When E.F. Hutton talks, people listen." Well, when Charley Lau spoke, people leaned in, and listened with squinting eyes and wide open ears.

Charley was such a student of the game and recognized so well the mind game between pitcher and hitter that Royals pitchers often talked to him about how to pitch to certain opposing batters.

BUDDY BLATTNER: "Charley Lau was the best hitting coach ever in the game. One of my most intriguing and amusing after-game dinners was one night with Charley Lau, Lou Piniella, and Hal McRae. Charley stood up with a napkin, in the middle of the restaurant, and demonstrated his approach to a swing. Then, Piniella stood up with a knife and fork and demonstrated his swing. I can hardly imagine what people thought."

McRae was Lau's first student with the Royals who understood what Charley was trying to teach. He went on to become the game's first true designated hitter. As a result of his work with Lau and his ability to grasp Charley's teaching, I've enjoyed talking hitting with Mac as much as anyone else in the game because he does an incredible job of breaking down the whys and the mechanics of hitting. It stands to reason that the St. Louis Cardinals sought out Mac to be their hitting coach after he had managed and worked in the front office for Tampa Bay.

Starting in 2009, the Royals hitting coach was one of the best-ever pure hitters the club has had: Kevin Seitzer. Much like George and so many other successful players in this game, Seitz, a fellow central Illinois product, wasn't considered a can't-miss prospect, even when he came up in 1986.

But Kevin played hard, ran hard and worked hard. He was the ultimate contact hitter, who could go to the opposite field or pull the ball, and occasionally had power. Overall, though, he was just a tough out. Much like Zack Greinke, Kevin was a baseball *player*. He loved the game and, I think, the nuances and camaraderie associated with the game.

Hal McRae's aggressiveness and fiery personality rubbed off on his teammates.

KEVIN SEITZER: "I was never expected to do a whole lot at any level I played. There were colleges that weren't interested in me, and didn't think I was good enough to play in their program. Then when I was in college at Eastern Illinois University, where I played three years, I hit .400 against Division I pitching, yet scouts didn't think I was good enough to go very far. When I was in Rookie ball, I wasn't good enough to get to A-ball; then I wasn't good enough to make it to double-A; then I wasn't good enough to make it to triple-A; then I wasn't good enough to make it to the big leagues. Once I made it to the big leagues, they thought I wouldn't stick. Eleven years later, they were all wrong.

"I don't disagree with some of the things they said, but they just don't know what's inside a person as far as work ethic, desire, focus, concentration and the will to win. I failed a lot in my career. This is a game where you can fail seven-out-of-10 times and be considered a pretty good player.

"My mindset was that I was going to see how far I could go. I was riding a wave. If I got to A-ball, I could tell my grandkids that I played pro ball. If I got to double-A, I could tell them that I made it to double-A, and so on. I was content at whatever level I was at. I had a very, very good foundation, or base, instilled in me with my dad growing up, and then with my coach at Eastern Illinois.

"My college coach, Tom McDevitt, really poured a lot of the basic fundamentals into me that when I made it to pro ball, I felt like I had a head start on a lot of kids. It wasn't so much the mechanics of the game, but it was the thinking, the mindset. One thing he kept yelling at me about was to stay within myself. He told me, for instance, that I wasn't a home-run hitter, so I should try to hit line drives. You should work at what you're good at, and stay within that when you go into the game.

"He also taught me to worry about what I could control. You can control your attitude and your work ethic, and the desire that you put into each game. Then, don't get caught up in everything that's going on around you. Do what you've got to do to get the job done. I never forgot those lessons. I called him many times throughout my career, and he had to yell at me again about those things because my thinking would get wrong. He always brought me back to where I needed to be."

Even though it'll be awhile before we know what kind of hitting coach Seitz will be, we do know that much of his college coach has worn off on him. Kevin's teaching is very much about staying within yourself and not trying to be something that you aren't. Another thing he really stresses is getting to know individual players on a personal level. When you look at former Royals who could become great hitting coaches, Kevin Seitzer would have to be at or near the top of that list, probably alongside McRae.

Before leaving the subject of hitters, though, this seems like as good of a spot as any to mention something about power hitters. The Royals haven't been known as a club with big power numbers. Because of the size of Kauffman Stadium and the way the ball has always carried (or not carried), the stadium hasn't been conducive to big home run numbers. Our first true power hitter, however, was Big John Mayberry. When the Royals acquired Big John from Houston in December 1971 for Jim York, the club had the home run and RBI guy it needed. Mayberry didn't disappoint.

He led or tied for the team lead in home runs all but one of his six seasons with the Royals. Big John played at Municipal for one season before we moved to Kauffman Stadium, which didn't have bigger dimensions, but it played bigger than Municipal, probably by about 10 feet or so. That might not sound like much, but to a home-run hitter, that can be substantial.

JOHN MAYBERRY: "As a power hitter, I could hit some balls real good and they'd go out. But I sometimes liked to hit balls on the end of the bat and they still go out. Not every home run has to go 450 feet. I liked to get some that went 378 feet. So that made a difference over the course of the year. But I've always thought that, over the course of a season, the difference between a home run and a line drive base hit is a fraction of an inch. Some years your home runs might be doubles and other years those doubles would be home runs. As long as you're hitting the ball hard and driving in some runs, that's the main thing."

Base Stealer

Characteristics and the role: The key to being an effective base stealer is knowing when to steal. That's the most important thing, along with knowing when not to steal. You have to have confidence that you can get a good jump and steal. The first step is critical — the most important, really — when stealing a base. You're not going to beat the catcher, you're going to beat the pitcher by getting a good jump. It doesn't matter how much of a gun the catcher has for an arm, he's pretty useless if the pitcher doesn't do a good job of holding the runner on base. You have to have a really good feel for what the pitcher's move might be. A lot of really good base stealers say it's easier to steal on a left-hander than it is on a right-hander. Why is that? The left-hander is facing you so you can see everything he does. The right-hander has his back to you, so he's essentially screening his first move from you. Most base stealers feel it's easier to steal third instead of second. Most base stealers feel it's easier to steal third on a left-handed pitcher than a right-handed pitcher.

We've had guys like Willie Wilson, who could fly. And John "Duke" Wathan, who perfected what they called a "walking lead." And then Amos Otis, who combined speed with intelligence.

With Duke, his momentum was already going toward second base, which made him faster. Willie didn't need the walking lead. He'd get a good lead and then rely on his sheer speed.

In 1982, Duke set the single-season stolen base record for catchers in a game at Texas.

JOHN WATHAN: "I didn't know this at the time, but the grounds crew had already decided that if I got the record there, the game would be stopped and they'd give me the base. From what I heard later, they had an old base at second to give me, and they had a brand new one at third. Well, I actually stole third against Frank Tanana and we couldn't get the base out of the ground. Bill Haller was the umpire at third, and after a few minutes of them not being able to get the base out, I told him to go ahead and start the game. It was kind of embarrassing to stop the game like that. He said no, and had the grounds crew come out to help. Eventually, they got it. I still have that base as a barstool in my house, signed by both Tanana and catcher Jim Sundberg, a good friend who I later played with in Kansas City.

"The record is special today. I still get people talking about it when they meet me, because you think of catchers as being slow, and no way could a catcher steal 36 bases in a year. I probably could have stolen more that year. I had 25 in June, and fouled a ball off my foot and was in a cast for four weeks. I came back five weeks later and got 11 more. I might have been in the 40s or 50s.

"I really think it's a lot tougher to steal a base now than it was back then. Pitchers then didn't use that move where they spin around to second, so it was a lot easier to steal third back then. That move never works today, but it keeps runners close. Coaches call more of the pick-off attempts from the bench than they did when I was playing. Plus, I had a way of walking off the bag, and if they didn't try to stop me, I'd keep moving. I took a real short lead, but as long as I had movement toward the next base, I could get a good jump. It was surprising to me how long it took teams to figure out what I was doing. Finally, after a few years, they'd yell as soon as I got on first base, 'Make him stop!' Then I was in trouble. I stole a few conventionally, but that move really helped."

Amos was right in between Willie and the Duke. He wasn't quite as fast as Willie, but he had a wonderful sense of how to steal. He really had probably the best sense mentally of how to steal of anybody we've ever had with the Royals.

AMOS OTIS: "I took the most pride in my base stealing. I made bets with my teammates, such as U.L. Washington. I would tell them that I could steal second base standing up against a certain pitcher. We'd bet a dinner with all the trimmings in the next town we visited. Then I'd steal a base, and would wipe the dust off my shoes. I usually could do that when I wanted to. I was pretty proud that out of 410 chances, I stole 340 bases. That's a pretty good percentage."

WILLIE WILSON: "A.O. would study pitchers. He'd say to U.L. and I, 'See that wrinkle?' What wrinkle? 'That wrinkle in his pants. When that's there, he's going home.' That's how he was. He'd find something on a pitcher that would give him away."

By the way, don't doubt that story about A.O. making those wagers and then pulling it off. Many of his teammates, including Frank White and Willie Wilson, have corroborated the story. Usually with a smirk and a shake of the head as if they wouldn't believe it, either, if they didn't witness it.

One of the greatest individual rivalries — if you want to call it that — that I've seen with the Royals involved Amos when he'd get on base against pitcher Vida Blue. Really, it started at home plate. Vida was a pitcher who relied on rhythm. If he got into one, he could be very tough to hit. To break that rhythm, Amos would step out of the box a lot or ask the home plate umpire to check the ball. Vida would get so frustrated, that, at times, he'd throw the ball directly to Amos.

On the bases, A.O. simply drove Vida to distraction at first base. Vida was a left-handed pitcher, so he faced first base when he worked from the stretch. Amos took the biggest lead against Vida that I've ever seen a major-league runner take against a major-league pitcher. Let's put it this way. Remember the dirt around the bases when Kauffman Stadium had artificial turf? Amos would oftentimes have both feet well onto the carpet! That's about an 18-foot lead. To this day, I don't know how Amos figured out how to get that type of lead against Vida. I guess that's a mark of a good base stealer.

Role Player

Characteristics and the role: People oftentimes mistake — or inter-change — the terms "role player" and "utility player." There is a differ-ence. Normally, a role player is a guy who's been in the big leagues for awhile and he's come to grips that he's not an every day player. He's never been, nor will he ever be, the team's superstar. A utility player, which follows this section, is a guy who can do a little bit of everything for a club.

A role player's mindset is such that he can play on a moment's notice. So, it's important that role players get in games to stay sharp, which some managers are better at fostering than others. Some guys are very good at coming off the bench to pinch-hit. As a player you've accepted that role and you understand what's expected of you to help the team win. Instead of bemoaning your fate, you center your energies on that job. If you do that, you'll be successful and will help your team-mates.

Whitey Herzog had a great knack for making all the guys on the ros-ter, including the role players, realize they were important to the team's success.

PETE LaCOCK: "One key for our club is that Whitey played his bench a lot. Every seven or eight nights, bench guys would play and stay fresh. And he had good bench people. No-name guys like John Wathan, Jerry Terrell, Joe Zdeb and I loved baseball and could provide value off the bench because Whitey kept us fresh."

The general manager and the manager work together to develop a team, and help to make sure that each guy has his own job. If each player concentrates on that job, he'll be more effective and the club will be more successful. If a manager doesn't work his role players and they end up sitting on the bench for 21 days, the odds of being successful are far less. It's not only a mindset, it's also about physically getting the repetitions.

The winning Royals clubs have had very good role players. In the 1970s, for instance, Whitey Herzog platooned Tom Poquette and Jim Wohlford in left field. That way, they could face the pitchers they'd be more successful against.

The same held true for the team that won the World Series in 1985. Although Darryl Motley was the Royals' main right fielder, Dick Howser also used Pat Sheridan out there. Sheridan was a left-handed hitter who could do a number of things well, although not necessarily great. He was a decent runner, could throw OK, was a solid outfielder, and good line-drive hitter. Dick could plug Pat in for seven or eight games and they wouldn't lose anything.

PAT SHERIDAN: "(Howser) was like the little general. He instilled in us that it was a business but we were going to get it done. I think he believed that. He was well respected, which isn't always the case. But he made sure guys knew their roles. The worst thing in any sport is to not know your role. We knew what was expected of us. Dick's job was easy at times because he had a good nucleus and he filled in the platoon players when he needed to. We had a strong pitching staff and a good closer. I've talked to John Schuerholz since my career and he's said you can't have a team of superstars. We had the George Bretts, Hal McRaes and Frank Whites who could carry the load, but we also had role players, which makes the manager's job a little easier. I was a role player. I know that. I think we all want to play every day but if you accept it and play the best you can in the major leagues, that's better than being an every day player in the minor leagues. I had always been an every day player, and it's easier because you're always in there and seeing live pitching. Being a role player wasn't my choice but if it was the only way I was going to stay in the big leagues, I was going to love it."

The other big role player on that team was shortstop Buddy Biancalana, who became somewhat of a cult hero that season thanks largely to late-night talk-show host David Letterman's "Hit-O-Meter." But Buddy, who didn't carry a big bat, was a solid defensive upgrade from Onix Concepcion, whom Howser benched late in the season.

Utility Player

Characteristics and the role: Different from a role player, a utility player is someone who can play anywhere he's asked. Jerry Terrell was the ultimate utility player for the Royals in the late 1970s. In many ways, John Wathan was a utility player because his managers could plug him in at catcher, first base and outfield. Dick Howser also could count on Greg Pryor as a solid utility player during the early 1980s. In more recent years, Esteban German was the quintessential utility player, who played in the infield and outfield for Buddy Bell and Trey Hillman.

When talking about a true utility guy, though, you have to start with Terrell. He had the perfect temperament for that. He accepted that role. He knew he wouldn't be an every day player, so he made the most of his ability and his willingness to play anywhere. He wasn't all that fast and didn't have a great arm. But he understood situations and he worked hard, always ready to go in.

Before joining the Royals in 1978, Jerry had played for the Twins, his home state and favorite team growing up. But when his agent told him that the Royals were interested, Jerry jumped at the chance, even though his playing time would be limited.

"I had been a utility player my whole career," he said, "and I figured with George Brett at third, Freddie Patek and U.L. Washington at shortstop and Frank White at second, I was going to be the guy who played behind the scenes."

That's the mark of a humble guy who knows his role and has accepted it. He didn't try to be what he wasn't.

Now, when we say Jerry did it all as a utility player during his career, *he did it all*. Literally. That includes pitching a couple of times for the Royals. He was always badgering Whitey Herzog to let him pitch. Well, Jerry got his chance against the Yankees in Kansas City. The Royals were down 17-3 in a particular game and Terrell came in to pitch in the top of the ninth inning. He ended up doing something that no other player — including Hall of Fame pitchers — can top. I'll let Jerry finish the story.

JERRY TERRELL: "When I went in the game, John Wathan came out and said, 'What are you featuring tonight, big guy?' 'Well, I gotta fastball, curveball, slider.' He said, 'No, you don't. Tonight you have a (batting practice) fastball. Just throw it in there and let's get out of here.' As he was going back to the plate, I kept thinking how I wasn't just going to throw BP.

"The first batter was Fred Stanley, an old teammate of mine in Minnesota. He was yelling at me how he was going to take me deep. I said, 'Chicken, you're not even going to get it out of the infield.' Duke called for a fastball, I threw it with a little cutter action on it and Stanley popped it up to short. The next batter was Bobby Brown, who was hitting left-handed. Duke called for a fastball away. I turned it over a little and Brown popped it up to Clint Hurdle in foul territory at third base. Two pitches, two outs. Lenny Randle was up next. Duke came out and asked what I wanted to throw. I said fastball. He ran back to home plate and Lenny said, 'You're going to drill me, aren't you?' Duke told him I was going to throw a fastball. For some reason, Lenny didn't believe him. I threw a cutter in on his fists and he popped it up to shallow centerfield. Three pitches, three outs. I got a standing ovation! They wanted me to do a curtain call. I wasn't going to go out for a curtain call...I'd get drilled by their pitcher. But Reggie Jackson was in the Yankees dugout waving a white towel saying they gave up.

"Marty Pattin was in our dugout with the other pitchers when I got in there. They stood up and walked out in unison. As they were leaving, Marty turned and said in a gruff voice, 'It ain't that easy.' I think he had given up seven earned runs in 1/3 of an inning that day. He didn't speak to me after that for weeks.

"The bottom of the inning I was hitting fourth. I got up there with a guy on base and singled to right-center. I got another standing ovation.

I hadn't had one in eight years, and I got two in just a few minutes. We lost 17-4 but there were about 30 reporters around my locker. They told me I set a record that day by being the only position player in Major League history who retired the side on three pitches. To this day, no position player has done that."

Jerry, who still has an upbeat personality, was always in a good mood it seemed. In much the same way that Hal McRae's aggressiveness and fiery personality rubbed off on his teammates, so, too, did Jerry's positive outlook.

JERRY TERRELL: "One of the toughest things on a ballclub is to stay in ready condition. If you don't play for 10 days to two weeks, it's tough to perform. But as a utility guy, you're expected to perform whenever called upon. Whitey Herzog and Dick Howser both were very good about rotating guys. Whitey made sure we got a chance so we wouldn't lose our timing. Batting practice is good, but it's not game speed. Whitey was very, very good at making sure we were game ready.

"On the mental side, the biggest thing for me is my relationship with Christ. He gave me the ability to play the game. For me to say I'm going to go out and do the best I can is to thank Him for what He gave me. So I always went out there with the attitude that I was going to do my very best. If I made an error, I wouldn't let it bother me. But, I figured I had to do that much better to make up for the error. If it might take a week or so before I had that chance again, I just had to be that much more game ready.

"But when I was playing the game of baseball, I felt no pressure. None whatsoever because I was thinking through scenarios ahead of time."

A guy who had that same type of personality was Jamie Quirk. During his 18-year big-league career, Jamie played every position except centerfield and pitcher. He was always up, keeping everybody else loose and engaged.

JAMIE QUIRK: "We had some great players in the '70s, but the rest of us were guys who were survivors and we had to out-think and be smart in the game because our abilities maybe weren't as good as everybody else's. John Wathan was that way. He was a very smart player. I like to think of myself in that category. Greg Pryor was a very smart player. We had a group of guys who knew, ability wise, that we had to have something on the opponent besides speed and strength and power. We had to out-think them. We had a group of guys who could do that. Whitey instilled that in us. He was a thinking man's manager, a guy that reminded us that we had to be not only physically better, but also mentally better than the other teams."

There's always been a certain irony to me about Jamie. When he signed with the Royals out of high school in 1972 as the club's first-round pick, he was headed to Notre Dame on a football scholarship. He was going to play quarterback for the Irish. Period. Physically, for the game of football, he wasn't equipped to play anything but quarterback. But, by choosing baseball, he ended up playing many different positions.

Clubhouse Leader

Characteristics and the role: Winning clubs need one or two guys who are willing to take on the role of clubhouse leader. The player — or players — who know how to motivate their teammates, can lead on and off the field by example, and aren't afraid to hurt anyone's feelings if a hammer needs to be put down behind closed doors. The person who took that role when the club needed it and ran with it was Hal McRae. Ask anyone who played with Mac and they'll tell you how important he was to the success of the Royals' best years, not only because of what he did on the field, but also what he added off it.

Only, it didn't actually start that way for Mac.

AL FITZMORRIS: "Hal liked to stir it up. Then he liked to get out of the way. Hal came over to the Royals from the Cincinnati Reds, but before he got here he had broken his leg in winter ball, and he could hardly walk. But all we heard about was Hal McRae and the 'Big Red Machine.' About halfway through the season, he was hitting about a buck-80 or .190, and we were on the bus from Milwaukee to Chicago. It was an hour trip, so we didn't fly. But McRae's chirping. John Mayberry was in the back and he shouted, 'Why don't you shut your buck-90 hitting mouth up! I'm tired of hearing all of this Big Red

Machine bull-.' Then he just started going after McRae and ripping him. 'You guys come to the American League and think you're going to have an easy time seeing breaking balls instead of fastballs. This is where you learn how to hit, in the American League. Anybody can go to the National League and hit fastballs.' He just kept going and going. You could see the veins in McRae's neck start to pop out before he said, 'That's it! I'm coming back. You might kick my butt, but I'm coming back.' Mayberry's just sitting back there, laughing. We had to grab McRae, knowing that if he went back there, it wasn't going to be good for McRae."

HAL McRAE: "I came from Cincinnati and we had a winning ball club over there. So naturally, you think you should win. If I brought anything, I brought the belief that if you're going to play, you should win. Pete Rose was on that Cincinnati ball club. And it was a good ball club. They all played hard. But I kind of took my lead from Pete. I enjoyed the way he played. ... Seeing Pete, I thought that was the way to play."

STEVE BUSBY: "Most of us as younger players — Splittorff, Amos Otis, Freddie Patek — were influenced significantly by Hal McRae. Hal had that 'Big Red Machine' mentality from being around Rose, (Joe) Morgan, (Tony) Perez, (Johnny) Bench and people like that. Baseball was not just a game to be played and taken lightly. It was a 24-hour a day — in the locker room, on the field, away from the ballpark — situation where it was competition. You had to learn how to compete at the major-league level and learn how to do it quickly and consistently. Hal McRae brought that drive, that inner-confidence that he knew what he was doing, and nobody was going to beat him, kind of attitude to us. Determination, hard work, and the ability to sit back and laugh at yourself when things go wrong, as they invariably do."

Again, part of the job of the clubhouse leader is to be somewhat of an enforcer. Hal needed to do that with a short-lived Royal named George Scott, who maybe thought he was more of a leader.

Scott came to the Royals in June 1979, 13 years in the league with Boston and Milwaukee. He came here in exchange for Tom Poquette. When George got here, he didn't really have anything left in terms of ability. His best years (and I think his post-best years) were behind him. Whitey Herzog mainly used George as a pinch-hitter or as a fill-in at first base.

George's nickname was "Boomer," which obviously didn't have anything to do with his voice, because he was Mike Tyson before Mike Tyson. There was nothing booming about Boomer's voice.

When George Scott got here, he wanted to wear number 5, which had been his number with the Red Sox. The only problem was that the Royals already had a player named George wearing number 5. And, by 1979 our George had established himself as a pretty good star.

Still, for the life of Boomer, he couldn't figure out why he couldn't have number 5. And he talked it up constantly … on the bus, around the batting cage, in the clubhouse, you name it. He probably said it in his sleep.

He'd say in that high-pitched voice: "I'm George Scott. I deserve number 5. Boomer gets no respect around here. I'm number 5." Yada, yada.

As a part-time player at first base, Boomer wasn't producing. In his only at-bat during a game, for instance, he'd come in with a chance to produce some runs, but he'd ground into an easy double play. It seemed he did that all the time. Then he'd go into the clubhouse and start chirping again about his number. "I'm number 5. I'm Boomer Scott. I've been in the big leagues for a long time. I get no respect."

On and on and on this went. Finally, about three weeks later, while Boomer's dinking balls to third base and hitting less than his weight of 215 pounds, he went 0-fer in a game. I believe he was 0-for-6, but we were in the clubhouse when Boomer started whining about his number again.

Finally, our enforcer, Hal McRae, whose locker was only a couple down from Scotty, snapped. He'd heard enough. He shouted, "Boomer, shut up! I'm sick and tired of listening to you talk about number 5. We have another number we're going to give you … 6-4-3." The room was silent. But, that worked.

We didn't hear another word from George Scott about number 5 for the rest of his time in Kansas City, which wasn't very long. In fact, Boomer, who wore number 0 here, fittingly, played in 44 games for the Royals before the club released him. The Yankees, of course, signed him and he played the final month of his career there.

Scout

Characteristics and the role: There are so many different types of scouts, but whatever the level, first and foremost, a scout needs a feel for the game. Is this player I'm watching just a good athlete, or is he a baseball player? Or, is this guy smart and can make a play to help us win instead of a play that will help us lose? The generic but critically important outside things.

But the toughest part of the job for a scout at all levels is scouting a player's head, his heart and his stomach. That's when you talk to other people — family, coaches and possibly other scouts. That, to me, is the genius of scouting. Pretty much all Major League scouts are wonderful at sitting down and picking apart a team for three or four games to determine who's playing well, who's throwing the ball well, and what mistakes they are making.

The Royals have had great scouts throughout the years, but the ultimate scout is 2007 Royals Hall of Fame inductee Art Stewart.

Art grew up in Chicago. When he was a kid, he enjoyed hockey as much as baseball. He'll tell you that he was a goalie without a mask. I told him one time, "Art, I look at your face and can tell that." We've had some laughs about that. He's still a very big hockey fan and watches a game or two a night. He was a solid baseball player, though.

ART STEWART: "I was running (an amateur baseball) club in Chicago called the Chicago Yankees. I went to Chicago Heights to see a pitcher and he got knocked out in the second inning. Well, here comes this 5-10 guy, who was cracking the bullpen. Many of the scouts who were there had left to go scout other games. But I started watching this kid and it turned out to be Jim Bouton, who would go on to write one of the best baseball books of all-time, *Ball Four*. He was going to

Western Michigan and I asked him about playing for our team in Chicago during the summer. That's how I ended up in scouting. I didn't know I was scouting but I ran this club and I was getting the best talent in the area. We were winning state championships and going to national tournaments. The Yankees approached me about scouting. I told them I was still playing and I didn't want to get involved in anything like (scouting). They told me I could run the club and still play for a few years before taking over the Midwest for them.

"Well, I made sure I didn't pitch Bouton around Chicago so the scouts wouldn't see him. He pitched in the small towns and at a penitentiary. Then he went to college and after a year other scouts became aware of him. He decided to sign the following Thanksgiving. I had the "in" with him because he was on my club and he knew me and his father knew me. We signed him over Thanksgiving dinner in 1958 at his house. Lee MacPhail was the general manager of the Yankees then and he gave the OK for a $25,000 package, which was a lot of money then.

"But as scouts, we're kind of the faceless men of baseball. We're behind the scenes, even though scouting is the life and bloodline of any organization. You have to find the players and sign the players."

Art has been with the Royals since 1969. His signings here have included Kevin Seitzer, Brian McRae, Mike Macfarlane, Bo Jackson, Kevin Appier, Mike Sweeney and Joe Randa.

ART STEWART: "Bo was the greatest athlete and player with ability that I've ever seen, and that includes Mickey Mantle as a kid. Bo had the most unbelievable talent. We rate players and 80 is the highest. That's All-Star projection. Bo was 80s across the board with unbelievable power, nobody could run with him, nobody could throw like him. He's also the strongest player I've ever seen. He broke a Cybex machine in the clubhouse one time. He certainly had the flare for the dramatic. It was unfortunate when he got hurt because he was learning how to play baseball. We don't know how great he would've been. The sad part is that he promised his wife that the NFL playoffs were going to be the end of football. His wife didn't want him playing anymore. Of course, the injury happened and his career was curtailed."

Two of Art's favorite signing stories revolve around two other former Royals outfielders, Johnny Damon and Carlos Beltran.

ART STEWART: "They were a dream in scouting because in scouting you never become a millionaire. Your biggest satisfaction is seeing guys when they're young and they become great players. Maybe Johnny and Carlos became beyond what we thought. They were exciting players and they were both interesting players. Johnny Damon was the longest marathon signing we ever had at 13 hours. Allard Baird was scouting Florida for us. I flew down there and we went 13 hours before we finally signed Johnny. Beltran was a question of whether we'd take him in the first round or second round. Some of our guys thought Juan LeBron was going to be the next Juan Gonzales. We went with LeBron and his big power in the first round. He never made it successfully to the big leagues. But we celebrated because when the second round came around, Carlos Beltran was still there and we took him. What a great young man. Both kids were great kids. They both signed out of high school. They both ended up on Broadway. They both are exciting players."

From Art you get tremendous excitement and optimism. He gets so excited when he sees a player he thinks can play at the highest level. His experience of being around the game for more than 50 years tells if a player has a good feel for the game — if he's smart, makes dumb plays, has a good concentration level, interacts well with his teammates. Art has experienced so many different things in the game. He's seen guys he was excited about and they didn't really pan out and others he might not have been excited about, but did some big things. He is a true scout, through and through. As of right now, he's in his early 80s. I think he'll stick around until he finds the next Bo Jackson.

Media Relations

Characteristics and the role: For a number of years with the Royals, as with many other clubs around Major League Baseball, the person who handled media relations also took on the job of traveling secretary. Even today, the media relations person wears a few different hats. He (or she) handles media requests for interviews and credentials, serves as a liaison between the media and the club's players and personnel, and is often a venting board for everyone from the general manager to the manager to the players. He's a confidant for those guys. Plus, he — usually with the help of his staff — handles the media guide, fan publications, such as the Royals' *Gameday* magazine, and puts together game notes before each contest for the media to use. Along the way, every now and then, he'll hear from fans looking for something media related.

We've really had some excellent, excellent media relations guys with the Royals, starting with the first, Bob Wirz. Bob, who's from Nebraska, was with the Royals from 1969-74, when he left to work for two baseball commissioners, Bowie Kuhn and Peter Ueberroth.

In 2007, Mike Swanson took over the club's media relations department as Vice President of Communications & Broadcasting. This might sound biased, but Swanee is one of the best in the business. That's common knowledge around baseball. He's so good at getting something out almost immediately. He'll have a stat before you even think about it — and it's a stat that will be meaningful, which means he has a great feel for the game and his job. He has a wonderful disposition, which you have to have for this job. You can't be volatile. You have to have an even personality. His judgment is wonderful in deciding what information to release and how to put out a fire here and a fire there. Frankly, he has all of the elements of a good media relations guy.

The really cool thing about Swanee is his background. It's wonderful. He grew up in Kansas City. His mom, Betty, worked for the Chiefs and A's during a 36-year career. And his dad, Bob, was friends with Roger Maris. Swanee cut his sports teeth with the Chiefs and A's, working in the equipment room, and then in the PR department with the Royals.

Former Royals PR guy Dean Vogelaar hired Swanee as an intern in the 1970s. Vogelaar was not a details-oriented kind of guy, which you need in that job. When Swanee was working for Dean and a mistake would show up in the pre-game notes or whatever, someone would ask Dean about it. He'd just say in his quick-speaking tone, "Oh, that's not right. Swanee (screwed) up." That became a running joke, even though, knowing Swanee, it probably wasn't true.

Swanee, who worked for the San Diego Padres, Colorado Rockies and Arizona Diamondbacks, is more than just a media relations guy, though. He's also one of the best statisticians in the country. He's worked alongside the best national broadcasters in the business including Keith Jackson, Howard Cosell, Al Michaels, Jim Nantz, and the team of Pat Summerall and John Madden. He's done stats for those guys and more at six Final Fours, six Super Bowls, four NFC Championship games, five Sugar Bowls, six Cotton Bowls, three Fiesta Bowls and the 2007 BCS national championship game.

He worked the longest with the legendary Keith Jackson, whom he calls "awesome." Matt Fulks included a great Swanee-Keith Jackson story in a column he wrote in 2007 for Kansas City's Metro Sports. It was a lesson for the young Swanee from the 1980 South Carolina-Georgia football game, which featured running backs George Rogers versus Herschel Walker.

Let's just say Swanson was out pretty late the night before the game and wasn't as sharp as he should've been at kickoff. Rogers wore number 38. Number 36 on the team was a kid by the name of Carl West.

A USC running back broke away for a 76-yard run. Swanson, not really listening to Jackson's call of the game, glanced up and saw what he thought was number 38. He quickly put together a note card that read: "12 carries, 157 yards and three touchdowns," and handed it to Jackson.

Jackson looked at the card and flung it out the window without missing a beat in his broadcast.

"All of a sudden I looked and realized that West ran the ball, not Rogers, and I thought, 'I've just lost my job,'" Swanson said. "I could tell Keith was really ticked at me by the way he threw the card out of the booth. During the break he told me that I screwed up.

"At the end of the game, when he was going through the credits, he thanked me on the air, as he usually did. I was shocked. I said, 'Why did you mention my name today? I was awful!'

"He said, 'That's why. I wanted the whole world to know who did the stats today.' He then went on to tell me that I was back the next week."

I love that story. And I love that Mike Swanson is in Kansas City. Even though it might not show to you guys as fans, we're really lucky to have Swanee running media relations for the Royals.

Traveling Secretary

Characteristics and the role: Details, details, details. Basically, the traveling secretary oversees everything in regard to travel. It's a thankless, stressful job where, if everything's going right, it's supposed to. But when it doesn't, you have to fix things in a hurry because 50 people or so might be counting on you. You deal with airlines, the truck company that carries the luggage, the bus company to move the team around when you're in a city, hotels, meal money, ticket requests, you name it. You might have a guy tell you that nine members of his family will be coming to a game or a series and he needs tickets for every one of them for each game. Someone might be unhappy about his room, so you have to fix that. When a player's traded, the traveling secretary deals with him to make sure he gets to the next city OK. If you're not attuned to detail work, you have no chance. On top of that, for awhile, the person who was handling travel was also in charge of media relations.

Things are made slightly easier today because we fly all chartered planes, so you're not beholden to a commercial flight. That wasn't always the case. In fact, one great traveling secretary for the Royals was David Witty, who made every road trip (81 games) a season for about 15 years. Many of Dave's stories were shared earlier in the book, but there's one more to show what kind of a pain this job of traveling secretary used to be. When he started in the late 1980s, we were flying commercial still.

DAVID WITTY: "Before I say anything about the job, put it in this perspective. How many times have you shown up at a stadium, or turned on the radio to hear Denny or turned on the TV to watch a game and you hear, 'Sorry, tonight's game is being postponed because the Yankees didn't make it to town'? Think about 40 years with the Royals,

162 games a year, and not one has been postponed because the Royals couldn't make it to another city or their opponent couldn't get to Kansas City. It's really amazing to think about that. In the early days, and we're talking 1987 when I started, we flew commercial flights. In my first year, we had 17 Eastern Airlines commercial flights. The way the arrangement was set up, the players had three seats for every two players, and we had a block of rows, for instance rows 11-22. There were a couple of times when we'd arrive, start to board the plane, and they wouldn't have the rows ready and passengers were already on the plane. Regular passengers would have to move around and then they'd be told that there weren't enough seats, since we had the center seat empty in each row. There were some pretty ticked passengers when that happened! On top of that, you're talking about a commercial flight, so if it was scheduled to leave at 10:00 or something like that, we had to be there on time. So if there's a rain delay or an extra-inning game, it caused some headaches. I remember at least twice in Milwaukee when we'd have to have police escorts to get to the airport in time. It took five or six years before we were flying all charters, which made life a little easier because the plane was waiting there and we would take a bus directly to the plane and get on.

"You think it's a hassle sometimes to arrange travel for just you and your family, think of doing it for an entire baseball team plus the traveling party. It was stressful at times, but we had fun on a lot of those road trips."

Dave has an amazing photographic memory. If you tell him your phone number once, he'll remember it seven months later without writing it down. If a player would say, "Hey, in two months, when we're in Cleveland, I need five tickets for some friends," he'd remember. He also follows college football so closely that he could probably give you the score for that South Carolina-Georgia game that Swanee was working with Keith Jackson.

Because of his memory and attention to detail, I don't think you could do much better than Dave when it comes to traveling secretary. He was perfect in that regard.

With Dave gone, the Royals now have a very capable traveling secretary, Jeff Davenport. But he wears two completely different hats as the director of team travel and the director of clubhouse operations, which means he oversees everything for the 25 players, coaching staff, manager and trainers in regard to all of their requests and needs at home and on the road.

Clubhouse Attendant

Characteristics and the role: This might be the job most boys (and some girls) who grow up as baseball fans in a Major League city want to do. You could also call it a batboy, ballboy, or, as they're known, "clubbie." Basically, these are the guys who take care of the players, from making sure uniforms are ready, to cleaning up the clubhouses before and after games, to getting water, bubblegum and sunflower seeds, to making sure there are baseballs for batting practice, to helping players put the balls on a batting tee. Pretty much everything they do isn't seen.

If you're a big baseball fan in Kansas City, you might be familiar with the name Chris Browne. He's worked in the front office for the other professional baseball team in Kansas City, the Independent League's T-Bones, where he's currently the General Manager. Back in 1985, though, when he was a teenager, Browne started with the Royals as a clubbie.

CHRIS BROWNE: "Back then with the Royals, you'd start in the visiting clubhouse, which was neat because you got to meet all the other guys coming to town, like Eddie Murray, Cal Ripken, Bert Blylevyn, and so on. After a couple of years on that side, you'd do a stint as ballboy and then go to the Royals side. And then you become the batboy. There were about four to six of us total, doing a little bit of everything.

"When you're not on the field and you're working the clubhouse, you'd go down to the dugout around the eighth inning to get ready to pack all of the equipment. I'm a kid and I'm standing behind the manager in the tunnel, just waiting. One time this didn't go so well was when Baltimore came to town with Earl Weaver as the Orioles' manager. Earl turns around, fidgety, and all of a sudden he starts screaming and yelling at me. 'Get out of here, kid!' I'd seen all of the run-ins Earl Weaver had with the umpires and I'd just experienced one firsthand. He wasn't much bigger than me, but I was practically bawling. The Orioles lost the game that night. I went in the next day and apologized to Earl, which is what we were taught to do. He said, 'You're all right, kid. I'm just a little superstitious and don't like people behind me. Next time you want to come down, you sit next to me.' I'll never forget that.

"Then there was the 1985 World Series. In Game Seven, you might remember that St. Louis pitcher Joaquin Andujar got thrown out of the game, as did Whitey Herzog. Buddy Bates was the equipment manager for the Cardinals. Buddy asked me to go down to the dugout and get Andujar's jacket and glove. This was during the game. I went down and got it. I gave it to Buddy and he handed me the jacket back and said, 'Here, kid, you keep the jacket.' I felt a little funny about it, but Buddy said, 'Go ahead and keep it, he won't need it next year, anyway.' My boss told me I could keep it. To this day, I still have that jacket."

Groundskeeper

Characteristics and the role: When thinking about these last three headings, it's obvious how lucky the Royals have been and how much the family atmosphere that was fostered here worked. We've basically had two groundskeepers in 40 years. For the past several years, it's been Trevor Vance. Before that (and even going back to the Kansas City A's) it was the legendary "nitty gritty dirt man," George Toma.

George was the groundskeeper by which all other groundskeepers in sports should, could and have been measured. In order to do this job, you need to be someone who, obviously, knows how to make a field look spectacular whether it's a grass or artificial surface. You need to know the best ways to prepare the dirt for your team. And, you need to keep track of potentially bad weather to be prepared and to keep the umpires ready.

The field was George Toma's baby, and he protected it that way. He has a wonderful feel for what he does and he's a perfectionist. Those might be the two biggest traits for a groundskeeper. When George was working full-time with the Royals, players would come in and say that the dirt is of such texture that you rarely get a bad hop. I used to go out and take ground balls during batting practice at Municipal Stadium, when I first started working with the team, and it was true that you never got a bad hop. It was a wonderful playing surface. Today's surface is certainly no exception with Trevor.

GEORGE TOMA: "I felt that every day I went to work, I had the best job anybody could ever have. You might hear a lot about George Toma, but there's no George Toma without the people I've worked with. When we were at Municipal Stadium on 22nd and Brooklyn, we didn't have any real equipment. All we had was one grass cutter and a tractor that was shared. I never had an assistant. The boys who made George Toma were the boys at Lincoln High School and Central High School and Paseo. Their mothers and fathers would bring them out to the stadium for a job. We didn't have the money that's out there today. We used to have to take cardboard boxes and broken seats down to Coleman's Junkyard on 18th and Vine, get the money, and then go down and buy seed. Then, when we went out to the two new, beautiful stadiums for the Chiefs and Royals, we still didn't have money. We planted a couple thousand trees but didn't have a way to water them. We worked hard at figuring out ways to get the job done — the kids were pioneers.

"I got one tractor to try and cut 65 acres. One day it didn't start and I was out in front of the Stadium Club, really complaining and kicking it, and a man comes out. He said, 'What's the matter?' I said, 'Look, our one tractor won't start and they expect me to cut 65 acres.' I had never met the guy, but he introduced himself and said, 'Don't worry, son.' He was good friends with Norm Cash, the ballplayer. Norm and I were close. His name was Hilton Hayes and he was with John Deere. People don't realize this, but when I was with the Chiefs and the Royals, I gave them $1 million worth of supplies. John Deere would give us brand new tractors every year. We also were given all of our sod and chemicals. I think this old man has put about $15 million into that stadium."

George isn't a very big guy, but he would get so mad when people would be on the grass at times other than during the game. Boy, he'd get ticked off. His famous saying was, "Grass grows by inches, not by feet." I always thought that was pretty funny. Then, he'd get so mad when guys would spit tobacco juice on the artificial turf. But he was completely married to his work and took a great deal of pride in it. He still does today as he works the Super Bowl locations and a couple bowl game sites. He's also worked during spring training for a few years for the Minnesota Twins in Fort Myers, Florida.

Here's how good George Toma is. Several teams tried to hire him away from the Royals. There were a few instances when players, such as the Yankees, took up a collection in the clubhouse to try and entice George. Luckily, he never went.

GEORGE TOMA: "When Alex Rodriguez was with Texas, he came up to me before a spring training game one day in Fort Myers and told me he wanted me to go to Texas to work. We talked for about a half-hour, and he said, 'All I want you to do is take care of the infield from second base to third base, and I'll pay you very well. After the game he came in and again talked to me about it. But I wouldn't do it because the (Texas) groundskeeper was a good friend of mine.

"He came up to me again (in 2007) in Fort Myers when I was working for the Minnesota Twins in spring training and the Yankees were in town. He asked me, 'What was George Brett's regime when he was hitting so well? What did he do before the games?' This that and the other. I said, 'You guys are going to Kansas City, just call George, he'll talk to you.'"

Much like George Brett, our other George, George Toma, is one of a kind.

Radio Producer-Engineer

Characteristics and the role: If you listen to enough radio broadcasts, you've heard one of us mention "producer-engineer Don Free" or "producer-engineer Ed Shepherd." Basically, these are the two men who have kept us on the air, game after game, since 1969. First, it was Shep, who died in 1992. Since then, it's been Don. It's remarkable to have just two guys — with the exception of the occasional fill-in — for more than 40 years.

A radio producer-engineer is responsible for hooking up all of the equipment, putting us on the air, keeping us on the air once we're there, and then going through the list of commercial spots and the commercial drop-ins during the course of a game. He's also in charge of the pre-game and post-game shows. We go down, record the interviews, and bring the recorder back to Don. He then takes it and slots it into the proper position in the broadcast. It sounds simple but it isn't.

If something happens during the broadcast and we're off the air, Don gets a call about it and he has to figure out why as quickly as possible. Of course, you have a gazillion wires going a gazillion directions. To troubleshoot like that when something happens is incredible.

Shep and Don are two totally different personalities, which is interesting when considering just the nature of the job and the technical nuances of it. Shep was one of the most well-rounded and possibly smartest people I've ever met in my life. He could do everything from helping you find a place to get beer in any American League city at 2 in the morning or taking you to his house and show you the piano that Count Basie used when he was learning to play.

Don, who's been with us since 1986, is a complete electronics wiz. It's pretty common for guys to bring electronic equipment to him before a game and ask him to fix it. I can't think of many times he hasn't come through in the clutch. If he can't, you might as well pitch it because no one can repair it.

Owner

Characteristics and the role: I want to end this chapter by looking at the job of a good owner. After all, in my opinion, the Royals have been fortunate to have had two very good ones with founder Ewing Kauffman and now David Glass. A good owner, in my opinion, is someone who obviously has the means to support a competitive team, but also the guts to hire people to do the job.

Ewing did just that. He wasn't a big baseball fan, but he hired the best baseball people he could find to run the club in 1968, the year before the Royals began play. From there, things ballooned with baseball people bringing in more baseball people. He trusted the people he hired to do the job they were hired to do. It seems like common sense, but how many times have we seen people buy a franchise or even buy any other type of business without a good understanding of it, and then constantly meddle?

Ewing was someone who cared deeply for every person who worked for him, as well as for the Kansas City community. There are so many examples of that, but one would be the Royals Lancers. The Lancers, who still exist today, are business people who are a volunteer sales force for Royals season tickets, and they also promote the Royals in the community.

HERK ROBINSON: "I couldn't say enough good things about Mr. Kauffman. I probably learned a hundred things from him. I started dealing with him one-on-one in 1990, when I was 50 years old, but I was around him a lot in the early days. By example, he taught us about treating people the way you want to be treated. Punctuality. Respect for others. He could bluff. He could be terse at times, but he would kid you about your mistakes. He had abilities to do so many things. He was a brilliant man, although he said he wasn't. When he was sick and in the hospital for a year, he read two books a day. I don't think, unless you're pretty intelligent, that you could or would do that. He was brilliant, but he'd just say he worked harder and did his homework. I think the characteristics he had were characteristics that anyone who's successful would have. I would hate to think (successful people) could have that level of success without the attributes that Mr. Kauffman had. He was a winner at everything he did."

JERRY TERRELL: "Mr. Kauffman was unbelievable. One year, we came off an incredibly tough road trip, something like 1-11. We were down in the dumps. Mr. Kauffman came into the clubhouse the next day to have a meeting. We thought he was just going to ream us out. Instead, he came around to every guy and gave us $100. He told us, 'That trip's behind you. I still love you guys. Take your wives out for a nice dinner and have some fun. Then let's get back out here and kick some tail.' That's when we went on a long winning streak, and then lost one, and then (went on another long winning streak). He just came down and shared his love for us."

In July 1993, Ewing Kauffman lost his battle with lung cancer. I don't know the details of his final hours, but I do know that one of the last conversations this wonderful man — who wasn't a big baseball fan, but bought a baseball franchise because of his love for Kansas City, and became a big fan of the sport — had was about the Kansas City Royals.

Fan's Question: How much preparation do you do for each series and how do you do it? With all the interesting stats and stories you've had over the years, you must have had a system that worked very well for you and the audience.

Carl Boles
Scottsdale, Arizona — formerly of Belton, Missouri, and a long-time listener

Denny: When you see players over and over, you know what type of player a guy is. From the team concept, most teams have tendencies. They have a character that you can usually expect. But you usually don't see that until about six or eight weeks into the season. Generally, though, before a series, you talk to people on the other club that you're going to play. Why are they playing well or poorly? Who's playing well or poorly? I go over the scouting report, which tells me the same types of things. Then, I usually feel well-prepared when we start a series.

HERK ROBINSON: "I think back occasionally to this. We had been trying to get Stan Belinda from the Pirates. Our scouts weren't terribly high on him, but Hal McRae was and Bruce Kison was. Belinda was darn good in Pittsburgh, and hadn't really gone downhill. I thought if we could get him, we could win the division. Some of our people didn't want to give up the players we gave up, which was a lot. We had a Lancers' dinner in Mr. Kauffman's suite one night and I called him at home at 9:00 to talk about Stan Belinda. He answered the phone and seemed so happy and at peace. He asked how the ballgame was going, asked what Lancers were in there and told me to tell them hello. We talked about Belinda and he said, 'Sure, if you want to do that, let's do it.' I got a call at 5:00 the next morning telling me that he'd passed away. That was the final deal that we made."

Incidentally, they made that deal — Dan Miceli and Jon Leiber to the Pirates for Belinda — on July 31, 1993. Ewing died the next morning, on August 1. Belinda played for the Royals the rest of that season and through the '94 campaign. "The deal didn't work out," Herk added. "Stan didn't get the job done. I don't know why he didn't, but he didn't."

Before Ewing passed away, his succession plan had already been put into motion. As mentioned earlier, David Glass was the Chairman of a board that ran the Royals while looking for an owner who would keep the franchise in Kansas City. A lot of people forget that David held that position before he ultimately bought the club. While he was Chairman of the Board, he tried to run the Royals as Ewing would've done.

HERK ROBINSON: "I'll always respect David Glass until the day I die, and I'll say that David was very conscious about not exercising a great deal of control (during the succession period) because he didn't want to make it look like he was setting it up for his eventual take-over. He was very, very conscious of that. Another thing I also admired him for greatly was when we had an opportunity to go to the National League. David and I felt it would be beneficial to do that since we'd be in the division with the Cardinals and the Cubs, and it was easy to envision a lot of positive things with that move. But David felt strongly — even though I think he was leaning that way — that, since he didn't have anything at stake financially, it wasn't fair for the ball club to make a change on something that Mr. Kauffman had founded and put in the American League. So, he backed off and said, 'No, it's not the right thing to do.' He may have had the authority by being the Chairman of the Board to do so many things that would've benefited him, but he didn't. David, in my experience with him, always did the right thing, every time."

I've always felt that if Mr. K could've handpicked the person to own the Royals after him, it would've been David Glass. Their business philosophies are similar and, like Ewing Kauffman, David Glass is doing everything he can to make the Royals a winning baseball team.

CHAPTER FIVE
WWDD — What Would Denny Do?

Baseball, by its design, is a wonderful sport of odd symmetry. Think about it: why is the pitching rubber 60 feet, 6 inches from home plate? Why not just 60 or 61 feet? Why are the bases 90 feet apart? Why that distance? But all of that is in the shape of a diamond, the properties of which can be classified as "flawless." The game of baseball is the perfect sport.

That said, however, baseball at the professional level has its share of flaws. So, with the other jobs and aspects of baseball out of the way with the previous chapter, it's now time for me to put on my commissioner's hat for a day.

Before we go on, I want to point out that I'm not saying I want Bud Selig's job. He's doing as well as he can with what he has to work with. We generally have Bud on during a game once or so a season, and he's always very candid and willing to answer whatever questions we pose to him. For the most part, Bud Selig is not the cause of all of the problems in today's game. Many of these issues started long before he became commissioner in 1998.

While working on this book, the editor mentioned to me — before he saw the Table of Contents — that he had an idea for a book after I retire: one on the current state of the game and what I'd change. (His thought was that it'd be easier for me to write that type of potentially

Bud Selig has been blamed for many of the game's problems, but several issues existed before he became commissioner.

offensive book when I wasn't involved with a Major League club.) Frankly, I'm not the only one who feels much of the following needs to change. Many are common complaints. Also, during the course of a season, you might hear me mentioning these on the air.

The Designated Hitter

This might be my biggest — or at least longest running — complaint in the Major Leagues. Please, end it! Get rid of the designated hitter!

The game of baseball was not designed to be played with a DH. The designated hitter was a gimmick that the American League stuck in there in 1973 because attendance was down. The league's pennant races weren't that compelling. The National League had the best players at that time, the 1960s and '70s, the best pennant races, the best teams, and the most exciting baseball. The interest in the American League wasn't great. So, what are we going to do? Add offense! Everybody loves offense, right? (Yeah, right.)

So, on April 6, 1973, New York's Ron Blomberg became the league's first designated hitter in a game against the Red Sox. There's a certain irony to the American League implementing the DH to bolster offense. A record 12 pitchers won 20 games that year.

I was willing to see what would happen in '73. I'll go a step further and say I was excited about the DH...in the first year. The concept was new and intriguing. I remember going into the second and third year of it, though, thinking how it wasn't that great. Then, after the fourth and fifth year, we started to see the difference in how the two leagues played. That's when I really didn't like it.

The American League style became a stand around, hit a home run kind of game. The Royals, with the influence of Whitey Herzog and the large artificial turfed then-Royals Stadium, which opened in '73, started playing a more National League style of baseball — running, speed, and pressuring the defense and pitchers to make things happen. That was Whitey's influence in a big ballpark. Teams like Detroit, Boston and Baltimore had outfielders who could hit home runs but they couldn't run that well. They'd come to our stadium and be lost, especially with the turf. Our guys were just spinning around the bases while the defenders were helpless. And we had great home records because of that. In fact, a scout said how the Royals played more like a National League team than any team in the American League. That was a compliment.

Every manager that I've talked to about the designated hitter has said emphatically that he would much rather manage without the DH. Especially the guys who have managed in both leagues. There's no hesitation, either.

In the National League, without the designated hitter, there is more strategy. It's more interesting. You are more in the game as a team, a player and a manager. A National League manager has more decisions to make. Frankly, it's a better game to me.

Having a DH certainly didn't hurt the Royals. After all, we had one of the best in baseball in Hal McRae, who joined the Royals in December 1972. But, it's reached a point where the "position" of DH can be a full-time hitter. Managers can pencil in a guy at DH who's a defensive liability but he just came out of the gym and he can hit a ball 816 feet. Not a lot of strategy there.

"I think the National League is more pure baseball, where you have better pinch-hitters coming off the bench and better bullpens," said former big-league pitcher Bill Gullickson, who spent 14 years in the Major Leagues with Montreal, Cincinnati, Houston, the New York Yankees and Detroit. "I'd rather face the DH four times than face a guy who does nothing but pinch-hits off the bench. The DH is mostly a power guy, so I'd have a better idea how to pitch him.

"As far as hitting, if I was winning, I enjoyed hitting. I didn't mind coming up if I had to bunt the guy over or something, but we generally weren't put in a position where we had to hit and drive a run in."

The only real difficult decision — if you want to call it that — for an American League manager is whether to pull a pitcher who might be on the verge of losing his stuff. In the National League, if the pitcher is showing signs of struggling and he's due to hit, it's a no-brainer for the manager. Pinch-hit and move on. His counterpart in the American League doesn't have the "luxury" of that decision.

In the late 1990s, the owners proposed the idea of ending the designated hitter experiment to the Players Association. The PA declined getting rid of the DH. I understand that...but that's too bad.

The Strike Zone...or Lack Thereof

Many fans have fought for years for the use of instant replay. (Although there's no truth to the rumor that the swell of support started in St. Louis after Game 6 of the 1985 World Series.) I don't believe in the use of instant replay by umpires during the game. Here's why: with all of the different camera angles today we can see instant replay on television broadcasts and we're reminded how good the umpires are. We see time and time again on plays that they're pretty darn good.

My major grievance with umpires is the size of the strike zone. Instant replay shows us that some of the umpires have a strike zone that stretches from a batter's belt to the middle of his thigh (so, I guess, instant replay is double-edged for the umpires). The size of the strike zone is one of the biggest flaws we have in the game today. It may be *the* biggest problem we have today. A small strike zone — smaller than what the rule book states — affects the pitchers' arms, the quality of the game, the pace of the game, and the interest in the game. Watching the pitcher and catcher play catch isn't very compelling. Not much happens in the game of baseball until the batter puts the ball in play.

Pitchers are at a big enough disadvantage today, and it's only getting worse with umpires who use a small strike zone. Hitters are bigger and stronger than they've ever been. Then, some of them, such as Barry

Bonds, add enough body armor that they could go for a joust with King Lear. That protection allows them to crowd the plate and get a better pitch. On top of that, it's a no-no to pitch too far inside without facing a warning and possible ejection from the umpire. The combination of those three things really puts the game into the offense's hands. Remember, it hasn't always been like that.

AMOS OTIS: "The only guy I ever thought tried to throw at me was my old Mets teammate, Nolan Ryan. In 1977 (the Royals) were battling the Angels for the division and he threw a fastball toward my head. I turned my head fast, but I heard the ball go buzzing by my left ear and I also heard it in my right. That's the closest he ever came to hitting me. I got him back, though, because I hit a home run off him later that game."

Incidentally, you might remember that Oakland pitcher Stan Bahnsen drilled Amos in the head in September 1976.

WILLIE WILSON: "The first time I got to face Nolan Ryan, I didn't know you weren't supposed to bunt off him. I was batting ninth, I squared around to bunt and foul tipped the ball back, and went down in the process. I looked up and he was standing over me and he said, 'Don't you ever (blankety-blank) bunt on me again.' I said OK. But I tried it again and fouled it back. Again, I went down, my bat went one way, my helmet went another way, and I'm getting up to collect myself. Nolan was standing there again and he said the same thing again. He hit me one time in my right thigh. The ball didn't bounce anywhere — it's like it just stuck to my leg and dropped to the ground. Being macho, I was just going to head to first. I took one step and needed the trainer. And that was from trying to bunt on him. Seventeen years later, when I was with the Oakland A's, I bunted on him again. It took me 17 years to do it, but I did. ... Nolan got respect. He'd throw at you, but he didn't want to hurt you."

Former Royals player Pete LaCock tells a similar story about the first time he faced Bob Gibson after coming up with the Chicago Cubs. Pete homered off Gibson. In his next at-bat, Gibson drilled Pete in the ribs. Pitchers can't do that anymore.

Combined with the idea that pitchers have to hit a small strike zone, a smaller zone means they're throwing more pitches. That, in the long run, affects their arms. Then there's the pace of the game, not necessarily the amount of time of the game, but rather whether there's a good rhythm to it.

Several umpires around the league need to re-learn (or, in some cases, possibly learn for the first time) the proper strike zone and stick to it during games.

Game Scheduling

Before leaving for spring training in 2009, I knew the Royals opened the season on a Monday afternoon in Chicago against the White Sox. Since hockey season would still be going on, I thought I'd check the schedule for the NHL's Blackhawks. Sure enough, the Hawks had a game scheduled for Wednesday night. In college, some buddies and I would go to Chicago on Sunday nights to watch the Hawks, which was a lot of fun. So, I figured the Royals and White Sox would play an afternoon game on Wednesday for their second game of the season, and then I'd make it over to the Blackhawks game that night. When I looked at the baseball schedule, though, I realized the Royals and White Sox were scheduled to play a night game on Wednesday, April 8. A night game!

It's perfectly fine that I'm missing a hockey contest for baseball. But, think about that: a night baseball game in Chicago in early April.

Why in the world are you trying to force a night game in early April in Chicago? I'm relatively familiar with Illinois weather in early April, so I'll guess that whatever the weather on April the 8th in Chicago, it's going to be more conducive to baseball on that afternoon than on that night. Isn't that a fair assumption? Who made that decision? Who said, "Hey, let's play a 7:15 game on Wednesday night, April 8th. It'll be beautiful."? Who gets the best in that deal, the players? The fans? Anybody? It makes absolutely no sense to me. C'mon, use your head!

That's a team decision; it's not a Major League Baseball decision. As an organization, you decide your own starting times. As commissioner, though, I think I would have to enforce a "common sense" rule for every organization. That could entail so many things, one of which definitely being scheduling. After all, believe it or not, baseball is a sport conducive to summer weather.

In 1979, the Royals opened the season at home on Thursday, April 5, with a night game against Toronto. (At that time, our night games started at 7:35.) That day was absolutely beautiful, sunny with a temperature in the mid-70s. Perfect. I distinctly remember it because I had to mow my lawn early that afternoon, which I normally don't do on the day of the opener.

Around 6:30, though, the wind shifted from the southwest to the northwest. I'm not kidding, the temperature dropped about 30 degrees between 5:30 and 7:35. By the time the game started, the wind was bitter. The bottom dropped out. The air temperature was 46 degrees, with a wind chill easily in the 30s.

The Royals had a huge second inning. John Wathan, the fourth batter that inning, hit a triple with the bases loaded. When those three runs crossed, putting the Royals up 3-0, it was as if somebody phoned in a bomb threat. The stadium just emptied because most people didn't come equipped for that blast of cold air. Wathan came up a *second time* — the 13th batter — in the second inning and flew out, ending the nine-run inning … and the chance for the vendors to sell more hot dogs. The crowd, which began at 37,754, was probably a tenth of that when the Royals eventually won 11-2.

The chances of having good baseball weather in early April in most Major League cities are a heck of a lot better in the afternoon than they are at night. That 1979 opener was a classic example. Why in the world didn't we play that afternoon? Kauffman Stadium would've been empty after the game, by 5:00 or so, and everyone would've enjoyed the opener in beautiful weather. Instead, nobody enjoyed the opener that night.

The other part of April game times is this: rain and snow postponements early in the season cause all sorts of problems later in the year with rescheduling. If you schedule a game at 1:05 in the afternoon and it's raining, you still could get the game in later during the day if there's a break in the weather. If you schedule a night game and it's raining, you're not going to start it at 10:00, so you'll have to postpone it. That causes scheduling problems later in the season.

You have more margin for error when you schedule day games, especially in early April. You have a chance, if the weather's bad, to get the game in if you wait long enough. If you have a night game scheduled, you're not going to wait until midnight. That doesn't help anybody. People have paid good money for those tickets.

Suspending Play

The rain/snow question leads perfectly to the next thing I'd change if I were commissioner for a day. I have a problem with baseball's rule of not suspending play early in a game.

For instance, let's say the Royals are playing the White Sox. It has started to rain in the first few innings. During those first four innings, some extraordinary things are taking place on the field. For just the second time in club history, two Royals players — David DeJesus and Alex Gordon — have hit grand slams in the same game. And, pitcher Zack Greinke has struck out all 12 batters he's faced. Then the rain picks up. Umpires decide to delay the game, but the rain doesn't let up. After a two-hour delay, it's obvious the rain isn't going to stop. So, they call the game. Since the game hadn't become official after five innings, it'll be replayed, from the beginning, at another time. Everything that transpired in those first four innings — the grand slams, Zack's outstanding performance — is wiped out as if it didn't happen at all.

Are you kidding me?

Once a game starts, even if it's three pitches, it's started. Period. If there's a delay, the game should be suspended and restarted from that point. How many guys have lost home runs and RBIs over the years? Too many to count. Games are suspended and resumed already for other reasons. Why not add the elements to that equation? Just pick the game up where it stopped. Granted, Zack might not even pitch in the resumed game, but it'd be 12 more strikeouts added to his season total. Same with the home run and RBI totals for David and Alex. If the game has passed the "official" point of the fifth inning, that's fine. Call it. Otherwise, just pick up play where it stopped.

Length of Season

The overall length of the season, starting with spring training and ending with the World Series, is *way* too long. Spring training games start earlier in March, postseason with the wild card is longer, and the length of games is longer. As a result, I think, players are getting hurt more often. For every second a player's on the field, there's a better chance of him getting hurt. But there's less of a chance of him getting hurt in a 2 hour, 30 minute game than a 3 hour, 30 minute game. Besides, the quality of play isn't that great late in the year with players who are exhausted from the ultra-marathon season. When you're playing baseball games past Halloween, you've gone too long.

Steroids/Performance-Enhancing Drugs

For decades, players have tried to find ways to get an edge, legally and illegally. Most of the time, it stayed out of the public eye. As records have fallen in recent years, though, we've become increasingly aware of the problem in baseball with steroids, growth hormones and other performance-enhancing drugs.

I don't condone players using these substances. If they feel they need it, though, and they're willing to risk their future health for today, that's their business. But I find two things objectionable about steroids and other performance enhancers: records and future salary.

One is how steroids have skewed baseball's records. Not to say anything about the Mark McGwire-Sammy Sosa home run chase or Barry Bonds' pursuit of Hank Aaron's record. (All alleged, of course.) But look at someone like former Baltimore player Brady Anderson. In 1996, Anderson became the first leadoff hitter in Major League history to hit 50 home runs in a season. There wasn't another year in his career when he hit more than 21. In his 15-year career, he hit a total of 210 homers. His body betrayed him shortly after 1996, as is the case with many guys. Then there are the guys who have finished second for various batting titles behind someone who was using. Think about them for a minute.

The other thing I object to with steroids is played out in this scenario. You and I are in spring training. We play the same position, we have equal ability, and both of us are trying to make the big-league club for the first time. We both have wives and a couple of kids to support. We both want to play in the big leagues where the monetary compensation is much bigger. You've been taking steroids for 18 months and I haven't. You get the job over me. Is that fair? I really object to that.

There's a certain irony to that scenario.

"Players' salaries are so high today that many of them feel that they need to take a performance-enhancing drug to increase their productivity. That doesn't make it right, but that's the way it is," said former Royals player Greg Pryor, who runs a health supplement company in the Kansas City area.

"I never considered taking steroids," Pryor added with a laugh, "because if I did my fly balls would have reached the outfielders instead of dropping in front of them."

True to his word, Pryor had 14 home runs ... during his entire career.

He brings up a good point, though. Some players who have been caught have pointed to the notion that the pressure of the big-money contract led them to performance-enhancing drugs. Just think back to Alex Rodriguez's public apology in early 2009. He said how he felt he had to do something to live up to his record-breaking contract with the Texas Rangers.

When someone asks me about my thoughts on steroids, the question inevitably comes up about whether these players such as Bonds and A-Rod or Roger Clemens should be considered for the Baseball Hall of Fame. Really, that's an individual opinion from the Hall of Fame voters. However they feel in their conscience to vote is how they should vote. All I know is that the records should not have an asterisk just because it came in this steroid/performance-enhancing era. That's silly. It is what it is.

Salary Cap

It shouldn't come as a shock that in baseball, without a salary cap, the rich have continued to get richer while the poor have continued to get poorer. When the Royals and the Yankees competed for American League supremacy in the 1970s, the payroll discrepancy between the two clubs was in the neighborhood of $4 million. You can compete with that differential.

Today, you're talking about differentials of $100 million from the richest to the poorest. It's absurd to think you can compete with that. The best thing for a small-market team under these conditions is for its players to play well. That's also the worst thing that can happen, because if the players are that good, they're going to be good enough to be recruited by bigger teams with deeper pockets.

Even some of those deeper-pocketed teams have found out that substantially raising payroll each year might not be the answer. As former Royals general manager John Schuerholz said in 2006, shortly after John's Braves publicly talked about lowering their payroll: "We went from close to $110 million to $80 million in one snap of the fingers. We decided that operating at a level that we couldn't support economically made no sense at all. We were the poster child for idiot savants of baseball as the club willing to spend $20 million more than we make. The Players Association and the agents were just rubbing their hands to take advantage of us. We decided we weren't going to be the fools any longer. We decided this is what we needed to build the team and this is what we can generate for income. And we've won three years in a row with that. We had to be more creative and rely more on our player development and scouting programs, even more so than we had in the past."

It's not a pretty picture. Revenue sharing, which has a certain Robin Hood philosophy, has been a big benefit to smaller-market clubs like the Royals, but it hasn't solved the economic problems by any stretch. Seemingly, the most logical way — yes, again, we're talking logic and sensibility in Major League Baseball — to fix the issue and create a more level playing field is with a salary cap. It has worked in other leagues. The NHL was the most recent to do it, but they had to burn an entire season to get one. People thought baseball should've done it when they had the chance with the season-ending strike in 1994. With the rich as rich as they are, I don't believe we'll ever see a salary cap in baseball.

Guaranteed Contracts

Some feel that a way for a team like the Royals to compete in today's baseball climate is with guaranteed contracts. That means you're going to pay that player the amount of that contract for the length of it, no matter what. Cleveland did it in the 1990s with their young talent and it worked. Overall, however, I think guaranteed contracts are very risky.

You're really rolling the dice, especially if that guaranteed contract is going to a pitcher. What happens if that pitcher blows his arm out? You're out millions of dollars. It makes a little more sense to give a guaranteed contract to a young position player. But, even then, you have to identify the player to see if he's motivated, more or less, to excel. Some guys want to excel no matter what they're making. The salary alone makes a difference to other guys. You have to weigh that. Risky.

In a similar way, and just as risky, in the 1980s, the Royals offered "lifetime" contracts to a few players. It happened after Ewing Kauffman — in an attempt to set up some type of succession plan to keep the Royals in Kansas City — sold 49 percent of the club in 1983 to Avron Fogelman.

Kauffman underwent surgery in 1981 to remove a benign tumor from his chest. Shortly thereafter word began to spread that Mr. K wanted to sell part of the Royals in the event something happened to him suddenly. After failing to find a local investor, Kauffman began looking outside of the area with some huge stipulations that would keep his community investment, the Royals, in Kansas City for years to come. Fogelman was involved in commercial real estate in the Memphis area, but he wanted to get involved with a Major League Baseball team.

Not long after joining the Royals, Fogelman introduced this idea of a "lifetime" contract to the sports world. In essence, it is how it sounds: a player would sign with the Royals for the rest of his career. The idea seemed intriguing, similar to guaranteed contracts, but it's somewhat risky. Ultimately, I'm not sure how it worked out or if it really even made a difference. Three Royals signed these "lifetime" contracts: George Brett, Dan Quisenberry and Willie Wilson.

The Wild Card

Baseball introduced its version of the wild card in 1994, the strike year. Seems appropriate.

The thought behind it was that baseball needed more excitement, more drama, more teams involved in the postseason to keep the fans' interest up. So, baseball went from two divisions in each league to three divisions and then a wild-card team to balance the playoffs.

People say it's exciting, but my big objection to the wild card is that it rewards mediocrity. Until introducing the wild card, Major League Baseball did not promote mediocrity. Now it does because the league can pocket a few more dollars each season. Look at how many times the wild-card winner has won the World Series. Since 1995, the first year it was used in postseason, four teams have won the World Series as a wild card. It happened three straight years, actually, 2002-04, with Anaheim, Florida and Boston. I'm sorry, but it defeats the purpose of the World Series crowning the best team in baseball each year. You aren't guaranteed of having the best teams over the six-month season playing in the World Series.

The wild card is a great position to be in during the postseason because you're not supposed to win. So, you go in loose and easy. The team that won 18 more games and had the best record in the league is under all the pressure, and a lot of times, they lose in a short five-game series. You're reducing the value of the best teams' six-month, 162-game effort. Why knock yourself out for six months and shoot to have the best record in baseball only to play a three-out-of-five playoff series against a team with nothing to lose?

There needs to be more of a reward for being the best team over the course of six months. If you want three divisions, fine. Eliminate the wild card and give the team with the best record a bye in the first round of the playoffs, while the other two teams face each other.

A week off, even that late in the year, can kill a hitter's timing. The Royals saw that in 1980. After beating the Yankees in the playoffs on a Friday night, the Royals waited in New York for three days to see if they'd be playing Houston or Philadelphia in the World Series, which began the following Tuesday.

WILLIE WILSON: "Once you get past a couple of days off, your timing is shot. People don't realize how important it is to play every day. When you sit that long, not going through competition, you're going to be slower than guys who have been playing. It hurts you. The Royals were better than the Phillies on paper (in 1980), but it didn't work that way."

You know what, though? A first-round bye today, instead of the wild card, gives the players some healing time and a better team is not susceptible to being upset in a three-out-of-five series. I'd rather have the time off and take my chances instead of facing a team that finished 17 games behind me in the standings. The lesser of two evils, in a sense.

Otherwise, cut the season short a month and play 140 games, which is still a lot of games. If the playoffs are so important, start them earlier and play them when the weather's decent. To me, the best teams have always been identified by the first of September. So, just get on with the playoffs.

As a baseball fan, I like to see the two best teams in the World Series. With the playoff structure the way it is now, most of the time, you're not going to get that.

Postseason Scheduling

Speaking of the postseason, another thoughtless decision by Major League Baseball is the start times for postseason games.

Maybe you, like me, remember fondly coming home from school in the middle of October to watch the playoffs. Or, maybe you would sneak a radio with headphones to school so you could listen between classes or even during classes. Or, maybe you used to take an extra-long lunch break from work to catch a few innings. That's the way it was. Everyone accepted and, for the most part, enjoyed it.

It was intriguing to figure out a way to check out the playoffs during the day. Yes, there were night games, but you could count on at least a couple of the games being played during the day.

In 1955, while I was in grade school, the nun at our Catholic school must've been a baseball fan. That was the year that the Brooklyn Dodgers beat the New York Yankees in the World Series, when Johnny Podres won the seventh game. We got to hear the last three or four innings of that in our classroom. Why do I remember that? Because our teacher found a way for us to listen to the game.

In recent years, baseball has phased out daytime postseason baseball because they're afraid that nobody's going to watch the games because of work. Part of the problem stems from the television networks wanting games in prime time. I hate to break this to anyone who'll listen, but if you're going to watch at all, you're going to watch whether it's 8 at night or 1 in the afternoon. If you're interested, you're going to find a way to watch it. If you're not that interested, you're not going to watch, anyway. With the Internet, if people want to watch a day game, they can tune in at work. Isn't that what people do during the NCAA basketball tournament in March?

The way it is now, every kid is going to be in bed, asleep, when a game in prime time ends. If you play during the day, kids get home from school and they can catch the last few innings. It's memorable and meaningful. It becomes fan-friendly.

Would you rather watch the first three innings of an important game or the last three innings?

From Interleague Play to Realignment

In baseball today, it's very difficult to get a rivalry going unless it's already established. You have the Cubs-Cardinals, Red Sox-Yankees and, to an extent, the Dodgers-Giants. Although not ongoing, the Royals have had some nice rivalries during their existence. The first two that come to mind are Oakland and the New York Yankees.

The A's were a great rival because 1.) They bolted Kansas City for Oakland, which left some pretty hard feelings from some fans, and 2.) They were the best team in the American League West throughout the first half of the 1970s. Most of the Royals players didn't necessarily care about the A's leaving Kansas City. A few guys played for both clubs in Kansas City, but that wasn't a driving force to beat Oakland. The Royals knew, though, that to reach the postseason, they'd likely have to surpass the A's. They did just that in 1976.

Then came the Yankees. The Royals knew that to reach the World Series, they'd likely have to beat the Yankees. So, the postseason series between the two clubs in 1976, '77, '78 and '80 were outstanding. But even the regular-season series between Kansas City and New York were marked by outstanding games and one-upsmanship.

There have been a couple of others, namely the Chicago White Sox and Texas. Besides that, there isn't another team I'd point to as a "rival" of the Royals. The closest we have now would be the St. Louis Cardinals.

That rivalry began in 1985 with the World Series, but remained dormant until the teams played each other again in their first Interleague matchup in 1997. Those games have been a lot of fun, but for a few of the Interleague years, we met only once during the season. To me, that doesn't make any sense.

I don't see any reason why the Royals and Cardinals shouldn't play more times during the season. I don't see any reason why the Cubs and White Sox shouldn't play more often — when it means something — same with the Dodgers and Angels, Yankees and Mets, Astros and Rangers. People want to see that. Figures for Interleague play have been outstanding. You still have matchups that don't mean anything because they don't mean anything. For instance, Florida and the Royals or the Royals and Pittsburgh. They aren't games that spark anybody's imagination because of historical or geographic interest.

When the Cubs visited Kansas City in 1998 and 2000, those games were eminently more compelling and interesting than having the Mariners or Angels come to town for a weekend. Unless there is some type of pennant race or a record on the verge of being broken, there is no reason a general fan in Kansas City would care about going out to see the Mariners for three games. Maybe the Cubs aren't the greatest example because of their enormous popularity.

At the same time, maybe they're a great example of the problem with Interleague. Including the 2008 season, the Royals have not played the Cubs since 2001. The two teams met for three-game series in each of the first five years of Interleague play. That's it. Fifteen games between the Royals and the Cubs. We've played Milwaukee (18), Houston (21) and even Pittsburgh (20) more times than the Cubs.

Interleague matchups have been great for the most part, but we're left with far from a perfect system.

What would be a "perfect system"? As you might've read in the book's Foreword by David Glass, in the 1990s, we were chitting and chatting during a game at Kauffman Stadium. At the time, realignment was a hot topic, and David was on MLB's realignment committee. So, if I came up with a plan for realignment, he offered to present it to Bud Selig and the committee.

The plan I developed can best be described as "regional realignment." In essence, we'd have four divisions of eight teams each. My apologies to people who say they're hard-core traditionalists, but the American and National Leagues would be eliminated, as would the designated hitter.

When I first designed this, Montreal was in the league and there wasn't a team in Washington, D.C., so I've tweaked things slightly. Otherwise, here is the plan that I gave to David Glass, who presented it to Bud Selig and other owners.

The Four 8-Team Divisions:

Kansas City	Seattle
St. Louis	San Francisco
Chicago Cubs	Oakland
Chicago White Sox	Los Angeles Dodgers
Milwaukee	Los Angeles Angels of Anaheim
Minnesota	San Diego
Texas	Colorado
Houston	Arizona
Boston	Cleveland
New York Yankees	Cincinnati
New York Mets	Detroit
Philadelphia	Pittsburgh
Baltimore	Atlanta
Toronto	Florida
Washington	Tampa
EXPANSION	EXPANSION

The Schedule:

- The season would go to 160 games to make it mathematically workable.

- 112 games vs. the seven other teams in your division, which equates to 16 games against each team. Eight at home and eight on the road.

- Of the 48 games remaining, a team would play six games against the eight teams in one other division. Three at home and three on the road against each of them.

- You wouldn't play other divisions at all in the season, but you'd play a different division each season.

The Postseason:

• The winning team in each division would advance to the playoffs.

• Based on records, the matchups would be 1 vs. 4 and 2 vs. 3.

• The two winners would play in the World Series.

This way you haven't really cut games out of the regular season (two), but your postseason doesn't drag on.

The Advantages:

• Teams would establish and re-establish natural and geographic rivalries, while creating new ones in the division.

• Playing for one title after an exciting pennant race. The league winner moves on. Period. There is no need for a wild card. Sure, with four divisions you're always going to have one that's stronger and maybe one that's incredibly weak. That's true in any sport, but it's cyclical. That's just how it works out.

• From the fans' standpoint, all teams and most of the players would visit each Major League city every three years. For instance, the Braves, Dodgers, Giants and Reds would be in Kansas City every three years, which gives those games more of a unique feeling. In turn, you're creating more of an event and more possible sellouts because the novelty is there.

• Fans would get to know players on teams in our division.

• As far as baseball and teams are concerned, this would bring about far fewer scheduling problems. The plan would drastically reduce travel expenses and players would be better rested, which translates to better play on the field and fewer injuries.

• In all cities, I believe, attendance would go up. You'd draw from different areas. The Cubs, obviously, are a big item in the Midwest, so they would draw well, consistently, at any of the other six cities in the division. There are a lot of Kansas City transplants in places like Chicago, Minneapolis and Houston so the Royals would be a regular draw in those areas and others. And, in the summer, you'd be amazed at how many Twins fans and Brewers fans would travel to Kansas City. It's always amazed me. And, if you're drawing from your geographical area in the peak summertime where there is interest, you're drawing not only from your fan base but also from Minnesota's fan base, the Cardinals' fan base, the Cubs' fan base and vice versa. It seems so logical to me. (Yes, I'm bringing up logic one more time.)

- Ultimately, you'd have great races with a balance of power because the only games in September would be against teams in your own division. That places more importance on those games.

The Extra Benefits:

- With this plan, radio and television outlets would be maximizing the number of games in primetime because most of the games would be played in your own time zone. That means a bigger audience, which means more revenue from sponsors.

- More kids would watch and listen because of the relatively local interest, so you're cultivating new fans.

- It would foster a lot of good, long-term, regional rivalries.

There you have it. There are so many reasons to do this. If those eight teams begin playing each other a lot, you're going to see some really, really good things in terms of rivalries, attendance and better baseball. Plus you'd have compelling races and games in the month of September. It would be a very good deal for the sport.

With baseball's unbalanced schedule now, it is true that you play teams in your own division more often. For most current divisions, that translates to four other teams. But teams with which you could develop natural, geographic rivalries are not there. Would you rather see the Cardinals and Cubs more often or Detroit and Cleveland? Which would give you more of a reason to become rivals?

The biggest complaint I've heard is that I'm too liberal because doing away with the American and National League would kill baseball's tradition. Look, I'm as traditional and conservative as anybody is, but the structure of the leagues went out in 1969 when expansion brought about the two divisions in each league. Before the American League expanded in 1961 and the National League in 1962, both leagues had eight teams. The best team in each league went to the World Series. That was the postseason.

Twenty years ago, saying American League or National League meant a lot. There was history and tradition on both sides, plus a big difference between the two leagues. With free agency and players switching leagues regularly, expansion, Interleague, and fewer stadiums using artificial turf, saying American League or National League doesn't mean squat. So, to heck with the National League and American League! It doesn't mean what it used to anymore.

The important thing here is the interest in territorial rivalries. If you don't think they mean anything or have any impact on communities, go back and read about New York with the Yankees, Dodgers and Giants. Look at the history and feelings behind those teams. The Giants and Dodgers had a great rivalry because they played good baseball, but also because they were in the same league or division. (Again, at that time there were eight teams in each league.) The Yankees were in that mix because they played the Giants and Dodgers a lot in the World Series. You always had that turmoil and debate in New York over which team is the best. The Dodgers and Giants could settle who the best is by playing each other 18 times a year. There was always something to talk about, which is what you want. Besides winning, that's largely what makes it fun for fans.

Expansion/Contraction

For the sake of my realignment plan, I wouldn't mind seeing Major League Baseball expand. The addition of two teams would be perfect. I've heard complaints about how expansion dilutes the talent pool. Maybe that's true right off the bat, but it's fleeting. As we've seen at other times throughout baseball's history, it all evens out. Especially now, with international players becoming so prevalent in the Major Leagues, talent shouldn't be an issue.

Bud Selig talks about how attendance around Major League Baseball has never been better. If that's the case — and you have to assume he's correct and truthful — then adding two teams would only make those numbers bigger. I don't think adding two teams would hurt the golden goose.

Conversely, there was a lot of talk a few years ago about "contraction," a fancy way of saying that Major League Baseball would close shop on however many teams. Minnesota, Montreal and Kansas City were the main three cities being tossed around as potential goners. Personally, I don't think Kansas City was ever in jeopardy of that happening. I believe the owners respect David Glass too much, and I think he would've fought it hard until it was resolved with the team staying here. Now, the sport is doing too well across the board to consider contraction.

Fan's Question: Over the years, the organization has had its ups and downs. As a home team broadcaster how do you reconcile what your own opinions are with what you talk about during a broadcast? How difficult is this process, if at all?

Trevor Worley
Springfield, Missouri

Denny: My approach has always been that you have to be as accurate and honest as you can be. I don't take it personally when we're losing because I had nothing to do with it. In the course of 162 games, you're going to have some interesting games, some exciting ones and some really dull ones. You just do with what you have. As a broadcaster, if you're only as good as your team is, you might want to check for another type of job. Along those lines, you can't be a one-way broadcaster. Meaning, there are two teams on the field. You can't see just one team. There has to be a balance. If we lose 7-2, it doesn't mean we're lousy. Maybe the other team played really well. You have to evaluate both teams that are playing and describe what you see, and don't get caught up in the other things.

The All-Star Game

The Major League All-Star game, because of the nature of it, is the best of all the major sports. It's an exhibition in the middle of the season for the greatest sport. Most people don't really care about the NFL's Pro Bowl. The people who do care about the NBA had to watch the 2008-09 All-Star game on a Sunday night on cable. Meanwhile, baseball's All-Star game is a tradition.

That said, it's also an exhibition. We'd be better served calling it an All-Star Exhibition. A spring training game is not a game, it's a workout. Same with the All-Star game. You don't have 44 players in a game during the regular season. But you do in an exhibition, the All-Star game.

So, I am totally against baseball's decision to give home-field advantage in the World Series to the league that wins the All-Star game. The contest shouldn't have any meaning like that. To the players, it's a privilege to be an All-Star. And it's a time that should be fun for them. Don't try to make a bigger deal out of the game than it is.

If you want to do something fun and unique, do what the NHL does. Have a skills competition. There's the home run derby already, but add some other contests in which the players can participate for some bragging rights. I know for a fact that the NHL guys have a fun time with that.

Just don't ruin the honor of playing in the All-Star game, and the somewhat relaxing couple of days that players can spend with their families in the host city by turning it into a meaningful game.

Commerce
Bank
Member FDIC

CHAPTER SIX
Denny's Dozen

Working for the same company in basically the same job for more than 40 years, you tend to learn a lot about yourself and others — really, about life. Those lessons in my personal instance are magnified when considering those 40-plus years have been in sports, which offers so many life metaphors at every level of competition.

As I've thought about my career and philosophies for this book, I came up with 12 attributes, goals or lessons that I've taken from baseball. Hence "Denny's Dozen." Some of these are common-sense virtues that we don't think about often. But all of them are things that each of us should strive for in our every day lives, whether in the broadcast booth, on the field, or at our work places, and with our family and friends.

Denny's Dozen

1: Perseverance can take you where you want to go

2: Respect others' opinions

3: Manage with love, manage with fear

4: Be prepared

5: Learn to rise to the occasion

6: Develop competitive fire

7: Just get along with people

8: Don't be afraid to take a chance or go out on a limb

9: Motivate yourself

10: Be a good listener

11: Don't try to be what you aren't

12: Always strive to improve

No. 1: Perseverance can take you where you want to go

From a baseball angle, you'd have to point to somebody like long-time Royal John Wathan, who was never viewed as a can't-miss prospect in the minor-league system. As the story goes, when they evaluated players at the end of the season, Duke was never a prospect for the big leagues. The organization continued to label him "NP," which means No Prospect. He was a good contact hitter and he had an ability to steal bases. But, he wasn't that fast, didn't have a very good arm, and couldn't hit for power. He was a nice minor-league player with some major-league potential because he didn't do anything great, but he did a lot of things very well. However, since his lifelong dream was to play in the big leagues, he kept plugging away until he made it. Whitey Herzog loved Duke because he could plug Duke in anywhere. And, he did. Wathan caught, played the outfield and first base. He wasn't a superstar but he wanted to play in the big leagues and he kept persevering until he reached that level. Look at how it turned out. He spent 10 seasons with the Royals, 1976-85 (the club's glory years), before doing everything for the Royals from coaching, managing, scouting and broadcasting.

Perseverance is an important quality in life and business, too. Very few people are successful because they did something once. It's those people who plug away year in and year out who build lasting businesses and successful lives.

No. 2: Respect others' opinions

There are some pretty bull-headed people in this world. We come across them every day. Not stubborn people, per se, but rather people who always insist that they're right. In business, in families, in sports, it's so important to respect the opinions of other people. It doesn't mean you agree with it or that you take it to heart, but you have to respect it. A perfect person who exemplified that idea was owner Ewing Kauffman. (Really, Ewing was a perfect example of so many good attributes.)

You could say he followed "Denny's Dozen" just in starting the Royals. He may have been one of the least obvious of people to bring baseball back to Kansas City after Charles Finley took the A's to Oakland after the 1967 season. Ewing was just a casual baseball fan, but he had the wherewithal to buy the expansion team.

Many businessmen, most of them Ewing's friends in Kansas City and many of whom were very involved with the A's, prodded him to buy the team. And then Ewing's wife, Muriel, put him over the edge. Muriel was the last one to kick him in the seat of the pants and say, let's do it. If he was a bull-headed person or didn't really care what people thought, I might not be sitting here writing this book because we might not have the Royals.

Then there was Ewing's grand idea to make the club better. As he had done in the pharmaceutical business, he wanted to find unique ways to improve the Royals. So, he came up with the idea of the Royals Baseball Academy. His thought was to take players with very little baseball experience — but were good athletes — train them through intense work, and mold them into Royals baseball players. He felt that guys who were great athletes, perhaps in another sport, could be turned into solid major leaguers. So in August of 1970, he started the Royals Baseball Academy in Sarasota, Florida, with long-time baseball man Syd Thrift as the academy's director.

Some of the baseball minds in the organization didn't think the idea had any merit, while others wanted to give it a shot. Everyone went with it because it was something that Mr. K wanted to try.

BUDDY BLATTNER: "Ewing invited me and my wife to spend some time with him on his yacht to pick my brain about the academy. We talked about the negative and positive factors. I said, 'I know you have the financial means to do this, and you are going to get 90% of the people who say it can't be done. You want it to happen, so why don't you do it? You might be unhappy the rest of your life if you don't do it. If you can afford the failure, for goodness sakes do it.' Several people around the organization told him to try it and he did. Things just didn't work out. Ewing was a little ahead of his time."

The academy was designed as a two-year program (including college), so a high school diploma was a must for a hopeful. During the morning, at Ewing's insistence, each player attended school at Manatee Junior College. He insisted that they take some speaking courses and some personal finance courses. He wanted them to be able to mingle in society, to talk to the press and to be able to handle their money. So the players went to college in the mornings, and studied baseball fundamentals for the remainder of the day.

During the academy's entire existence, a lot of people continued to tell Ewing that it wouldn't work. In his own way, he listened to what they had to say, but continued to put money into it. Finally, in April 1974, the Royals Baseball Academy closed. But, as it turned out, the Royals got their middle infield of the late 1970s and into the 1980s out of the academy: Frank White (the academy's first and best "graduate") and U.L. Washington.

HERK ROBINSON: "Mr. Kauffman was a very hands-off owner. The only thing he ever really got involved with was the academy. He felt the minor-league system's rate of getting 4 percent of players to the majors — only .3 percent were legitimate stars — was a joke. No business in the world is successful that deals with those numbers. But, he said, 'Instead of messing up that perfect system, I want to try something.' He didn't cut any of our scouts or the number of clubs we had or anything in development, but he formed the Baseball Academy. Eventually, the academy sent 12 players to the Major Leagues, which showed that there was success in it. But it was very costly. Probably more expensive to get somebody to the Major Leagues that way than it was through the traditional method."

Besides Frank and U.L., one of the other graduates of the academy was Ron Washington, who played in the majors a few years, but he's gone on to become a respected coach and manager at the big-league level. He was a bench coach in Oakland for several years before becoming manager of the Texas Rangers. And it's all because of the academy.

RON WASHINGTON: "I was 16 years old, and had just graduated from high school (in 1970). Syd Thrift signed me for the academy from a tryout camp in New Orleans. We had 156 guys there, and I was the only one signed from it. The first tryout, he sent me home early. Then he called and invited me back with three other guys. I enjoyed every minute of (the Baseball Academy). We learned baseball on the chalkboard and then took it to the field. We learned to play together and play fundamental baseball.

"I learned perseverance through the Baseball Academy. It taught us not only how to play the game, but also how to be men and how to deal with adversity. We even went to school. I got a year and a half of junior college.

"The Kansas City organization was the only one I had been with and they traded me to Los Angeles in 1976. The knowledge that I give to the kids today, I learned it at 17 years old with Kansas City. Some of these kids don't have it yet. Mr. Kauffman did a great job of trying to do something for kids that might not get drafted. I guess it wasn't cost-effective, because they cut it out after two years. I thought it was a great idea, though. I was able to apply what I learned in Kansas City to the Los Angeles Dodgers. My game was applied in L.A. with everything I learned in Kansas City."

While we're on the subject of Ewing Kauffman and Herk Robinson, who started with the Royals as Assistant Scouting Director in December 1969 before eventually becoming the General Manager in 1990, there's another story that I find interesting that goes along with respecting the opinions of others. It's how the conversations between Ewing and a Royals GM worked when the GM was thinking of making a player transaction.

HERK ROBINSON: "I'd meet with him periodically and tell him what we had in mind and what we wanted to do. Or if I had a special thing, I'd go over and tell him what I'd like to do. That's the way the Royals' GMs always handled it with Mr. Kauffman. Typically, Mr. Kauffman would challenge you to the Nth degree. He would do everything in his power to get you to back off. He didn't want to hear, 'Well, you may be right on a couple of those things but I'd like to make the deal.' He wanted to know that you were as committed to that as if it were your own money.

"One time I wanted to sign Danny Tartabull for one more year when he was a free agent. Dennis Gilbert, his agent, said he'd sign for one more year. I went in to see Mr. Kauffman when he had gotten to the ballpark. I told him I wanted to sign Danny. (Here's what Mr. K could do to you.) He said, 'Well, can we win the pennant with him next year?' I said, 'Yes, we can win a pennant *with* him but I don't know if we can win a pennant *because* of him.' He said, 'If we can't win a pennant *because* of him, why do we want him?' As far as Mr. Kauffman was concerned, second place or 88th place didn't make a difference in baseball or in life — it wasn't first. I said, 'I think we can improve the club.' He said, 'Well, improving is not good enough.'

"'Well, if we get a couple other players...' I started to tell him. He said, 'What if you don't get those couple other players? Will you get your money back on Tartabull?'

"He was asking questions that were obvious and redundant. We went round and round for about 10 or 15 minutes. About halfway through, he slammed his fist down on the table in his suite, his pipe went flying about a foot and the ashtray with the pipe ash went all over the place as he said, 'I don't want to improve the club, I want to win!'

"Later in this conversation, he said, 'Go ahead and do it if you think it's the right thing to do.' That's the way he was generally. He'd do everything he could to talk you out of a deal without saying no, but if you would battle him and not back down, he'd eventually break into a smile and say, 'Go ahead and do it. I think it's a good idea. I like that, too.'"

You know, I think we sometimes forget or take for granted what an incredible man Ewing Kauffman was to everyone around him, and for the Kansas City area.

It's important to respect others' opinions and ideas. They just might have a better idea than you, maybe even be a little smarter.

No. 3: Manage with love, manage with fear

As a leader, these two go hand-in-hand because you have to figure out the personality of your people and know how to handle them individually. Good managers will get it figured out when they get to know the person. Some people react better to a pat on the back instead of a kick in the fanny. Good managers have to know when to apply what. We've seen in baseball that the good managers have a knack for that. Sometimes, nothing said is the best ploy. That's the knowledge and experience of the manager and knowing that person. Bad managers kick their guys in the fanny when they need a pat on the back and vice versa.

A good manager is able to instill the feeling in you that you can do this, whether the task is fairly simple or complex. He gives you confidence and he'll leave no doubt in his mind — or yours — that you can do it. If a manager can do that, then the recipient thinks how you don't want to let him down. That's the way my dad was. He gave you confidence to do something. You didn't want to let him down. A manager-player relationship is like a father-son or father-daughter relationship.

Joe Gordon, Bob Lemon, Whitey Herzog and Dick Howser all had a great feel for knowing what tactic to use and when. They were easy to play for because they treated you as a grown man. If you showed them you were immature, they could come down on you pretty good. But otherwise they were arm-around-the-shoulder, encouraging, positive, a mental boost.

In baseball, this idea of managing with love and fear isn't relegated only to the manager. As in life, in baseball it applies to any position in which a person has direct reports.

JOHN SCHUERHOLZ: "Mr. K was a hands-off owner, but his aura was always around us. We knew we couldn't disappoint Mr. K. We knew what he expected and the confidence he had in us. It never swayed from his viewpoint. Sure, he was aggravated when we lost, but never dismayed. He'd say, 'win with dignity and lose with grace.'

"I made the deal (in 1982) that blew up in our face that brought Vida Blue to our organization. He and a couple of our other players got caught up in the drug scandal in 1983 as a result of the introduction of drugs into our clubhouse, and we found out from the FBI and federal drug people that drugs were introduced (in the clubhouse) by that player that I made the deal for, Vida Blue. We had to manage our organization through that chaos and through that thunderstorm of negative circumstances. Every day, I had a meeting in the clubhouse with the media. I answered questions every day about how the Royals would deal with it, how we'd go forward. I told them how we were embarrassed and how it was a kick in the organizational stomach (I really meant groin). We worked our way through it. We worked through it because we had the unwavering support of Mr. K.

"After I made this horrible deal and after these horrible circumstances befell our organization, as we were working through it, one day (Kauffman) called me to his office. I thought that was it for me in Kansas City. He sat me down across from his desk, and with his steely blue eyes, said to me, 'Look, we made you general manager of this team because of our confidence in your ability to operate this organization effectively, making good decisions, and showing leadership. I do not want you to pull in your horns and lose your aggressiveness because of this trade. That's what makes you who you are.' How many owners would say that? Now you know why I have such admiration for Mr. K."

Indeed. Managing with love, managing with fear.

Successful leaders of businesses and organizations understand that you can get away with managing with fear for a short time, and maybe even achieve your goals. But managing with love is the hallmark of long-lasting success. You attract more bees with honey than you do with vinegar.

No. 4: Be prepared

It's the old Boy Scout motto, but it's also vitally important in our lives. I've always thought it was hard to be over-prepared. I always try, before a game or a series, to have more stuff in case I need it late in the game. It's called being driven by fear. It's impossible to be over-prepared, but very possible to be under-prepared. Once you're in the comfort zone after preparing, the confidence creeps in that says you can do it, which is a good mindset to get the job done.

Who ever built a fortune or a great life by "winging it?" I think we can agree preparation is the one constant to sustained success.

No. 5: Learn to rise to the occasion

Confidence, mental toughness, accepting the challenge all have to do with rising to the occasion. Experience helps, but obviously you're not going to have experience the first time you try something. So, confidence and mental toughness go hand in hand. If you accept the fact that you're at home plate with the game on the line or at the free-throw line with the game on the line, you have confidence. You have to eliminate self-doubt and compartmentalize it. Butterflies are good because it means you're getting prepared.

BUDDY BIANCALANA: "The (1985) World Series was a fabulous experience for me, as people can imagine, but taking it to a different level, that was the best baseball I had ever played. I reached a level of concentration that I never experienced prior to that time. I don't know how I got there except that for the first time I acknowledged fear — the fear that I experienced prior to game one of the World Series.

"I'll never forget sitting on my chair in front of my locker prior to the (first) game, about a half-hour before ABC wanted us (to line up) on the foul line. I started thinking, 'Oh my, this is really intense.' I figured I could put on my street clothes and go watch the game on TV somewhere, or I could grab my glove, walk down the runway and take the field. Obviously I'm glad I made the choice that I made."

As you may remember, Buddy went out, played solid defensively at shortstop, and batted .278 with 2 RBIs and 2 runs scored. So, Buddy, we're also glad you made the choice that you made.

"Rising to the occasion" may be different for an athlete than it is for a busy mother or a VP of Sales. But ordinary people do it all the time – they do their best when it matters the most.

No. 6: Develop competitive fire

Never give up on a play or the task at hand. I think the great example of that is golfer Tiger Woods. He never gives up on a tournament, a hole or a shot. Keep going until the game is over and the task is finished. You don't know how it will turn out. If you give up, you'll fail more often than not. Another great local example, regardless of your affiliation, is the 2008 Kansas basketball team. The Jayhawks trailed Memphis by nine points in the national championship game with 2:12 remaining. Of course, they catch up, Mario Chalmers hits that incredible 3-pointer and Kansas goes on to win the game in overtime.

Speaking personally, I am more competitive in baseball, football and hockey than I am in golf. I'm more accepting of a mediocre shot in golf than screwing up in another sport. At times, though, on the golf course, if I'm not playing well, the fire will come out. I don't take it away from the golf course. Everybody has his or her own degree of competitive fire, depending on the situation. But, almost everybody is competitive in one form or another. Being competitive makes things fun. It makes you want to do your best.

AL FITZMORRIS: "That (competitiveness) is what we were about. After a few sodas or something after a game, if I'd given up a homer that cost us the game, Amos Otis might come up and say to me, 'By the way, Fitz, how did you hold that fastball?' We'd live it, let it go and move on to the next day because all we thought about was winning ballgames. From about 1973 on, every city we went into, when it said K-A-N-S-A-S C-I-T-Y across our chests, everyone knew who we were, they were concerned with us and then afraid of us. We were so proud to wear that uniform. It was unbelievable. I get chills now talking about it."

STEVE MINGORI: "We lost a game one time that we should've won. Cookie Rojas went in the clubhouse and dumped the whole food table over. He then chewed the whole team out. That's what type of team we had. We eliminated mental mistakes to where we knew we were going to win."

Former pitcher Steve Renko, who's basically a lifetime Kansas City resident and who ended his career with the Royals after the 1983 season, knew about the competitive fire that the Royals were going to give him every time he pitched against Kansas City.

STEVE RENKO: "When you faced the Royals, you thought about two things — Willie Wilson's speed, because he was going to get on, and George Brett coming up to the plate. Hal McRae was a good hitter. Then, every once in awhile, a guy like Fred Patek would jump up and bite you. I remember a game in Boston when he hit two home runs off me, when I was with the Red Sox. The Royals were a true team. Somebody in that lineup was going to hurt you that night, along with George."

No. 7: Just get along with people

You should try to be as cordial as you can. Try to work within the framework of who you're dealing with. All types in business. Have a good feel for the people. Frankly, it doesn't hurt to have knowledge of what people are like before a meeting. The ability to get along with people takes you a long way. You can cultivate that and get better at it.

No. 8: Don't be afraid to take a chance or go out on a limb

If you think you might want to try something, do it. The one biggest example from my life is going out for football in college at Illinois Wesleyan. I didn't play in high school but it worked out great in college. One of my fraternity brothers, Vic Armstrong, who was Wesleyan's starting quarterback, suggested I try out for football. I did and as it turned out, it was a life-changing event. I got to know some of the people around the athletic department and I had a very good first season as a wide receiver. Because of all of that, they let me broadcast basketball that winter, which started my broadcasting career. Nothing ventured, nothing gained. I don't know how many times somebody thinks they want to try something and talk themselves out of it. You never know, you might be pleasantly surprised with how it might turn out.

Think of all the great businesses that were started on an idea that seemed crazy at the time. If you really think about it, if nobody ever went out on a limb, we'd still be living in trees!

No. 9: Motivate yourself

There are two types of motivation: self-motivation and the motivation we get from external sources. It's probably better to be self-motivated because that way you're not relying on someone else. The most successful people are self-motivated and they only draw a little from external forces and external motivations. It's amazing what some people do when they're told they can't do something. As the saying goes, 'Whether you think you can or you think you can't, either way you're right.' In Canada, there's this thing called "Hockey Night in Canada." While watching that, I saw a story about a hockey player up there who has only one hand. I'd say he's self-motivated to play hockey. How many people told Freddie Patek he was too small to play in the big leagues? How many people told Jim Eisenreich that he would never play in the big leagues after he'd been diagnosed with Tourette's Syndrome?

FRED PATEK: "The first year I went to spring training was 1966 in Daytona Beach, Florida, with the Pittsburgh Pirates. When I got off the plane, there were two guys waiting for me. These guys have cards with them and they're checking off all the players they're waiting for. I'm about 5-foot-3 and weigh about 120 pounds at the time. A guy named Bob Zuk had signed me. Jimmy O'Toole of the Pirates looked at his card, looked at me and said, 'Man, that guy did it to me again.' The card had me listed at 5-foot-8 and 165 pounds. That was my first experience in pro ball. It all worked out, though.

"It was like anything else, or any other professional player. It doesn't matter how big or small you are, you just have that mindset that you can do the job. I never thought of it in those terms, of being small. We're never going to see another small player in the big leagues. The one thing when I think about that is I was told all my life that I'd never make it. I wouldn't play 162 games. I wouldn't sustain the travel. Inner-inspiration says 'I'll prove you wrong.' That's what drives most athletes. That's what drove me. Plus, I always thought I had to work a little harder. I thought they were looking for a reason to get rid of me.

"The thing that's still special to me is the fact that I played for so long when I wasn't supposed to make it at all. People tell you all your life you can't do it, and you do it for almost 14 years … that's pretty good."

Freddie's middle infield mate for several years, Royals Hall of Famer Frank White, also was a very inner-driven person. The thing he did before each series wasn't to psyche the other guy out, but it was Frank's way of adding some motivation in his mind.

FRANK WHITE: "As a player, you need that desire and pride that says, 'I want to be better than you.' When I played, I wanted to be better than Willie Randolph for that 3-game series against the New York Yankees. I wanted to be better than Detroit's Lou Whitaker for that 3-game series, or whoever was playing my position for the other team in that particular series. So, before the first game of each series, I'd walk up to the other team's second baseman and tell him that I was going to out-play him for that series. I think that's why I became who I am."

Most of us don't have a fiery manager or a cheerleader around every day to get us going. You've gotta motivate yourself. So use whatever passion burns brightest for you, then go out and knock 'em dead.

No. 10: Be a good listener

For whatever reason, God gave us one mouth but two ears. Maybe we're supposed to be listening two-thirds of the time. When you're talking, you're not really learning anything. You're not advancing your knowledge. It's important to listen because you might gather some knowledge. I've seen interviewers a lot of times have a set of questions they want to ask a subject. No matter what the reply is from the person they're talking to, they're going to get that set of questions asked. If you're truly listening, you might want to go completely away from your questions. The same holds true for our day-to-day conversations. Buddy Blattner used to tell me when we started working together that he hated if I wasn't listening when he was doing his innings. He didn't like it if he said something on the air and then I came on and repeated the same thing. "You have to listen to me very carefully and I'm going to be listening carefully to you." He sure was. Listening is very important. Besides, if you're not a good listener, it's rude. Being a good listener is similar to respecting other's opinions, but just because you respect someone's opinion, doesn't mean you're being completely attentive to what they're saying.

ART STEWART: "Cedric Tallis, the Royals first general manager, was a great guy for getting the best scouts he could to scout the opposition. Plus, he was a great listener. Dayton Moore has a lot of Cedric Tallis in him. He takes opinions from a lot of people and then when it comes to making a deal, he digests those opinions and makes a decision. Cedric had good people evaluating. He weighed all of the input and then made the decisions."

Buddy Blattner was a great broadcaster and teacher. I was lucky to share the Royals broadcast booth with him during my early years.

No. 11: Don't try to be what you aren't

This is similar to the idea in an earlier chapter about knowing your role, whether that's as a star player or a bench guy. This, also, is the flip side to not being afraid to go out on a limb. Once you're on that limb, don't think that you can fly off. Going back to Buddy Biancalana, he was not going to be a power hitter. He was a singles guy. Period. Another example is Wally Bunker, the first person to throw a pitch in Royals history.

Here are a couple of humorous Bunker stories. Wally was a guy who could throw — in fact, he threw a complete game for Baltimore in the 1966 World Series — but he had a lot of

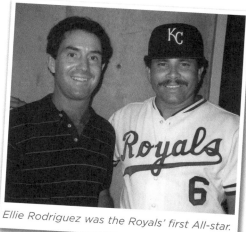

Ellie Rodriguez was the Royals' first All-star.

shoulder problems early in his career. But, he was the Royals opening-day starter in both 1969 and '70. It was evident early in 1970 that he might not being throwing as hard as he once did. His first pitch against Oakland was a fastball for a called strike. The A's lead-off hitter, Bert Campaneris, turned to Royals catcher Ellie Rodriguez and said, "Wow, I've never seen a pitcher lead off the game with a changeup." Bunker knew the end was near. He went 2-11 that season.

The next year, he was on a rehab assignment at Omaha. The O-Royals were playing against Tulsa. Wally started a game and the first batter, "some kid," as Wally calls him, led off with a hit. The next night before the game, this "kid" came up to Wally and said, "Oh, Mr. Wally Bunker, I'm so proud I got a hit off you. Can you sign this ball for me?"

As Wally says, "I went home and told my wife Kathy, 'That's it; I quit.' I was only 25 but I was finished."

Wally knew his limits.

No. 12: Always strive to improve

That's pretty obvious. Motivation becomes a part of that, as does not being afraid to ask questions of others. If you stop improving, you're basically standing still. Try to improve in all aspects of life. An athlete in any sport has to multi-task. In baseball, you can't be a one-dimensional player and survive. In hockey, you have to do different skills. Some facets you'll do very well. Other facets you don't do well, but you strive to get better in what you don't do well. You won't improve if you're only working on what you're doing well. That's hard work — not a lot of fun because there's adversity tied in with it. The key is being motivated enough, taking enough pride in what you do, and having enough desire to improve. If you don't work on the things that are more difficult, then you're spinning your wheels.

George Brett was not a Hall of Fame type player when he arrived in Kansas City from Omaha. He started to show promise in Omaha, which is mainly why they chose to bring him up, but he had to work hard to become a Hall of Famer. We've all heard the story — and read it earlier in the book — about how George and Charley Lau started working together to improve George's hitting. Well, people don't realize that George had to work extremely hard on defense. He may have had to work harder on his defense than on his hitting.

Fan's Question: It's always refreshing to hear your broadcast of a Royals game because you don't have some goofy catch phrase for every play on the diamond. You let the game happen and call it as you see it. Having said that, how do you know exactly what to say when there is a key play in a critical game? Think back to 1985 – the most exciting year in Royals history – when there were so many critical games that year, especially in the playoffs and World Series.

Brian Spano
Lee's Summit, Missouri

Denny: Obviously, you don't know when a great play is going to happen, but in much the same way a player would, you anticipate what might happen. Then, as the play is unfolding, I have a decent idea of what's happening. When that talking "Denny Matthews Bobblehead" came out a few years ago, it brought back a lot of memories of the final out call in 1985. As you recall, Game 7 was basically over well before the ninth inning. So, I just started counting down the outs as they happened. Then, when Darryl Motley caught the final out, it was obvious what to say in that moment.

I have seen guys get to the big leagues and year to year they get better and better. I've seen other guys who came up and four years later they're not better. And other guys come up, and they're skills decline in just a few years. Many guys don't put in the work to improve, and they end up not having long careers. It's easier to get to the big leagues than it is to stay there.

An entire industry has been built on the idea of continuous improvement. Successful organizations realize that you can't just "get it right" one time, then rest on your laurels.

You have to work to improve every day, every month, every year.

CHAPTER SEVEN
Oh, The Things I've Seen

W hen you've been broad-casting baseball for 40 years, you see plenty of both good and bad at the games and away from the stadiums. Here is my list of some of the good and the bad.

Best Royals Player: My answer has always been that I would go to the ballpark to watch Willie Wilson run the bases, Frank White play second base, George Brett hit, John Mayberry or Bo Jackson hit a long home run, Dennis Leonard start and either Dan Quisenberry or Jeff Montgomery finish it. That

Morganna, the Kissing Bandit, was a "big" hit around baseball in the 1980s. She would run onto the field and kiss players. I got a visit from her in the broadcast booth at Exhibition Stadium (appropriately enough) in Toronto.

would be a great day at the ballpark. You could see some great skills. We've had so many good players in Royals history that it's impossible to pick just one.

Most Significant Game in Royals History: The third game of the 1985 American League Championship Series against Toronto. We're not in the World Series against the Cardinals without that win in the playoffs. If we don't beat Toronto in Game 3, we're down three games to none. Essentially, we had to win that game because we'd already lost two in Toronto. If you lose your first game at home after dropping the first two on the road, you're pretty much dead. The odds are overwhelmingly against you. The Royals would still be without a World Series championship if it weren't for Game 3 of the playoffs against Toronto. That also was the best game of George Brett's career. George willed himself to lead the Royals to a win. Do you realize how rare it is for a position player to dominate a baseball game that way? It's possible, obviously, for a pitcher to control a game. It's extremely hard for a position player because, defensively, he can't control how many balls are hit his way and he's going to bat four or five times, tops. However, Brett did all of that.

George made huge plays at third, plus he homered twice and doubled twice. The Royals won 6-5. To me, that was George's best moment, his biggest moment, and most important moment at that time in Royals history.

Fan's Question:
Ginger or Mary Ann?

Harry Scott
Kansas City, Missouri

Denny: Actually, I'll throw one more in here. In answer to your question, I'll say Ginger (Tina Louise) because she would be the girl I'd constantly date and take to the prom. But then there's Morganna, the Kissing Bandit, whom I would take to the fraternity party on Friday night. I met Morganna in the mid-1980s at — appropriately enough — Exhibition Stadium in Toronto. When she targeted the Royals, Morganna would always go for George Brett and me, or me and then George Brett, depending on her schedule. So, it was always a doubleheader with Morganna. No pun intended.

Most Insignificant Game: Any spring training game.

Best Pitched Game, Both Teams: One of the neatest, most fun games I've ever broadcast was shortly before the All-Star break in 1976. It also remains one of the best-pitched games with a fantastic match-up. It was the Royals veteran Dennis Leonard against Detroit's flamboyant rookie, Mark "the Bird" Fidrych, who had a great sinker. It was a nice, hot summer night at Tiger Stadium. The place was packed with an overflow crowd. Fidrych was the hot item in baseball that year and everyone wanted to see him pitch. You had the feeling from the outset that this game could be something special. And it was. Fans hung on every pitch because each one meant something. Not many baseball games give you something compelling like that. Even though the Tigers had the off-the-wall "Bird," no one realized the extra fire that was burning inside Leo. See, a few days earlier, manager Whitey Herzog told Leonard, a Brooklyn, N.Y., native, that he wasn't going to be pitching against the Yankees in New York because he was going to be on the All-Star team. Oops. As it turned out, Herzog was mistaken and he told Leonard about it before the Detroit series. Leonard got worked up the night before pitching in Detroit and decided he was going to prove that he should've been on that All-Star team. Leo and the Royals won that game 1-0. Including postseason games, that mid-summer game in 1976 remains one of the most electric contests I've ever broadcast.

DENNIS LEONARD: "You always want to play for your hometown team, so before the Mets came into existence, I was a Yankees fan. When the Mets came into existence, it was a lot easier and safer to get to Shea Stadium. At that time (the 1970s), we had a lot of position players that made the All-Star team. In 1976, we had four guys. Shortly before the All-Star break, we were playing in New York and then Detroit. Whitey told me that he was going to hold me back because I made the All-Star team. In that particular year, Al Fitzmorris had a great record, Paul Splittorff had a great record, Doug Bird was starting and he had a great record. I was 9-2 at that point.

"I remember telling my dad that I wasn't going to be pitching (at Yankee Stadium) because I made the All-Star team. He told everybody, so I'm thinking cool. Well, P.S., Whitey apologized to me saying that he didn't know what happened. So, I went from being a big, tall stud, to feeling like a worm.

"My father-in-law, God bless him, flew to Detroit to meet us. We were in a little piano bar, I was drinking water, and I told him, 'Fidrych my [butt], I'm going to beat him tomorrow.' During the game, we had a runner on third, and Hal McRae hit a grounder to deep second base to score a run. We won the game 1-0. It was one of those situations where we were determined."

That's me with Dennis Leonard, who I think pitched one of the best games I've ever broadcast – a 1-0 win over Detroit – right after we were mistakenly told he had been selected to the All-star team.

Sadly, as we were finishing this book, Mark Fidrych died at age 54. He wasn't on the baseball scene for very long, but he sure left a lasting impression.

Most Inspirational Game: While we're on the subject of pitchers, specifically Leo, he was at the center of what is probably the most inspirational game I've seen. The game was an early season contest against the Toronto Blue Jays in 1986. This is a game that could go in so many places in this book because of what Leo went through to get to this point. It might be best to let him set everything up, starting with the game at Kauffman Stadium in 1983 against Baltimore that eventually led to this inspirational game three years later.

DENNIS LEONARD: "Cal Ripken was up. When I threw the pitch, I thought I got hit by a line drive originally. As I was going down, I heard the umpire call strike. The next thing I knew, my knee was hurting a little bit. I reached down and felt my kneecap on the outside part of my leg. I pulled it back in and the rest was history. Until I saw a replay of it, I never realized my body went the opposite way on my follow through. I imagine when I saw it, that's when it hurt the most. Really, the pain was instantaneous. It wasn't a continual pain. The doctor was poking at my leg in the clubhouse, and it was like jelly. I had no clue at the time what the prognosis was. The doctor was being nice to me and he said, 'Well, maybe you'll be back by August.' Well, three years later... It was just one of those things. Hey, it happened. I wish it didn't, but it did.

"I had three future surgeries on my knee with a very calculated rehab. That was the tough and boring part.

"I missed the 1985 World Series. I had a chance to pitch two innings that year, which was a boost to me. I sat on the bench in Kansas City for the first two games of the World Series. When the Royals asked me if I wanted to go to St. Louis with the team, I told them, 'Nope, I've got to go to Florida to rehab my knee, but I'll be back.' It was one of those situations where I was part of the team, but I wasn't a part of the team. Whether they lost or won, I didn't throw a pitch to change anything. So, I was sitting in an oyster bar in Sarasota when the Royals won the Series. I had a blast. I will cherish the ring, but it would shine a lot brighter if I was part of it. Still, that ring is very special.

"I wasn't even supposed to pitch against Toronto (in 1986). Danny Jackson was supposed to start the game. On the last day of spring training, he was running and twisted his ankle on a sprinkler head in the outfield. I was supposed to start the season as a reliever and work my way into the rotation. All of a sudden, I'm starting a game at home on national TV. I didn't want to embarrass myself. I wanted to go five good innings and do the best I could. The way the game was going, I was thinking, 'Wow! Please score a run.' We finally scored the run.

"In the ninth inning, the Blue Jays had a runner on base. Usually fans don't boo when a pitching coach comes out of the dugout. Gary Blaylock, our pitching coach, came out to the mound and got booed. He immediately told me they were keeping me in the game. I told him I could do it.

"There were about 27,000 people there that day. I really appreciated the applause and everything I received from the fans. I think the people knew in Kansas City that I was going to do everything I could to get back. With each operation, obviously my chances were getting slimmer and slimmer. I was on a five-year contract and I felt like I had to give everything, because I loved playing baseball in the big leagues. The way the fans reacted, and the little updates in the paper here and there during my rehab, I had a good feeling after that game there was an appreciation by the fans that I was able to come back.

"As I've said a lot, it's kind of weird, but with the fans' reaction and the feeling in the stadium that day, that was my World Series. I never worked that hard between starts in my life, from that game in 1983 to my next start in 1986! If I had any guts, I would've quit after that Toronto game. I told myself that it wouldn't get any better than that. That game was a storybook ending to three years of misery."

MARK GUBICZA: "A game I wasn't involved in, but will never forget was seeing Dennis Leonard make that unbelievable comeback and getting the shutout against Toronto. ... I watched him battle back from the knee injury. As time has gone by, I realize how difficult it is to rehab and come back. He went for a few years rehabbing that knee. Then to come out and throw a shutout in your first game against an incredible team like the Blue Jays. That was one of the most amazing days of my life."

A cool thing about that to me was watching Leo's family in the last inning. I had spotted them in the stands during the game. In the last inning, with each out, I'd look at Audrey and the kids. It was such a neat feeling to see them get emotional with the rest of us, and to think about how special that moment must've been for them after the hell Leo went through to get to that point.

Best Stadium (Not Named Kauffman): Wrigley Field for obvious reasons. The field, the charm, the history, the age of the ballpark. It's old-time baseball and it hasn't changed that much. The atmosphere inside and outside is fantastic. The Cubs have made the most of that ballpark. Fantastic job of marketing. They've almost given the feeling of a pilgrimage to a holy shrine. I thought Fenway was equally charming until they started messing with it, which diminished the charm. The Cubs have resisted all of that. It's pure baseball. There's nothing wrong with pure baseball. You can hear batting practice from outside Wrigley. You don't hear loud music. You're listening to the sounds of baseball. A lot of organizations have lost track of that to "entertain."

One morning during a trip to Chicago, John Wathan and I went out and walked all around the ballpark. I took a bunch of pictures. It was about 10 in the morning. Then, another time, in the early 1990s, the Cubs were in town playing the Pirates and we were in town playing the White Sox. The Cubs were playing during the day, so I went over, got tickets next to the dugout and sat there as a fan for most of the game. That was the first time I'd sat in Wrigley Field since working on my demo tape in the 1960s.

Best Uniforms: St. Louis Cardinals

Worst Uniforms: Probably those clam digger shorts the White Sox wore in, I believe, 1976. A close second would be the Houston Astros rainbow uniforms.

Best Organization (Excluding Royals): Baltimore in the 1960s and '70s. In the National League, I'd say St. Louis. They've been consistently good for years. Those two organizations cover all aspects from the field to fan accommodations to marketing to, well, everything.

Best Manager: Tony LaRussa, who's won in both the American League and the National League.

Best Place for Day Baseball: Wrigley Field, hands down.

Best Place for a Night Game: I'd say Texas. You could say it's the best place to have to play night baseball because it's always so hot down there during the summer days.

Funniest Thing Seen on the Field: This won't seem funny at first, but it's probably a fight our guys had in the bullpen area in Oakland in 1976. The two teams had some bad blood

I think Tony LaRussa is the best manager in baseball. He's in St. Louis now, but he's won in both leagues.

between them as the Royals were trying to knock the A's off the top of the American League West. Late in this one game, after there'd already been a skirmish at the mound when Dennis Leonard hit Don Baylor with a pitch, there was some type of commotion down by the Royals bullpen. I don't know what set off that little melee, but all of sudden two or three fans and a couple of Royals were pushing and shoving.

Then, the fans started coming down the aisle toward the bullpen area. A fan would run down, stick his head over the railing to get a better look, and get whacked. It was like a guy sticking his head through a hole at a carnival and getting hit by a water balloon. Then somebody else would come down, and he'd get the same treatment. At some point during all of this, Hal McRae grabbed an umbrella from one of the fans and hit somebody over the head with it.

Of course, the next morning's Oakland newspaper had that bullpen raucous pictured on the front page with McRae holding this umbrella, about to hit someone. Hitting coach Charley Lau was always getting on Mac because his top hand was dominant on his swing — he was rolling his top wrist over too soon. We were at breakfast the next morning, and Charley pointed to the picture in the newspaper of Mac about to hit a fan over the head with an umbrella. Charley, in his quiet way, looked at Mac and said, "See Mac, I keep telling you, too much top hand."

Best Prankster in Baseball: Moe Drabowsky. Baseball has had its share of practical jokers. The Royals alone have had some great ones. Earlier I shared some of Steve Mingori's stories. Bret Saberhagen was a good one, too. Drabowsky, though, was the most infamous in all of baseball. Drabowsky, who lost a battle with cancer in the summer of 2006, played in Kansas City for both the A's and the Royals.

A few months before he passed away, Drabowsky shared the following story with Matt Fulks. It's one of my favorite Drabowsky stories, and one of his favorite pranks. It happened at Municipal Stadium in 1966, while Drabowsky was pitching for the Baltimore Orioles. By this time, he had already pitched for the A's. In fact, this was Moe's first trip back to Municipal.

MOE DRABOWSKY: "Since I didn't speak with a number of my former teammates before the ballgame, I was going to call them during the game. I'd have to call and make sure that (equipment manager) Al Zych could call a rib place and make sure we'd have them in the clubhouse. I also had numbers for Charlie Finley's box, the radio booth, bullpen and dugout.

"Jim Nash was shutting us out with about a three-hitter. I dialed the Kansas City bullpen and Bobby Hoffman, their bullpen coach, answered. I shouted, 'Get (Lew) Krausse ready in a hurry!' Then I hung up. Krausse started warming up feverishly. We were doubled over in laughter. It looked so funny because Nash was just cruising. I let Krausse throw for two or three minutes, and then I called back and said, 'That's enough; let him sit down.' I called back a few minutes later and told them it was me.

"One writer said that I deserved one more victory on my record because Nash saw that bullpen activity and he got so flustered that he lost his concentration. That was not true. Nash beat us. But my fan mail definitely increased substantially after that story got out.

"With the Royals, we used to have a security guard outside the club-house door, and he sat out there with a shotgun. I said, 'Hey, Dick, give me that shotgun and I'll make sure we don't lose tomorrow.' He didn't give it to me. We kept losing and I kept asking Dick for the shotgun. Finally, he gave in. He took it down to make sure there weren't any shells in there. I walked in the clubhouse with the shotgun and said we needed to win. I then went out and gave Dick his gun back. I saw it needed 12-gauge shells, so the next day I brought 12-gauge shells. I put them in my locker under a towel. We lost again. I told Dick to give me his shotgun. He made sure there were no shells in there again. I walked in and said, 'Someone has to pay. Let me think about this.' Guys are showering down and in various stages of getting ready to leave. I popped two shells in the shotgun and said, 'OK, Chuck Harrison. Somebody sent you that voodoo doll in your locker that dangles. That's putting a spell on us.' I pointed the gun at the voodoo doll. I made sure no one was around because I didn't know the exact spray pattern of a 12-gauge. I pulled the trigger. BOOM! Clothes went flying out of his locker! There aren't too many characters in the game nowadays. Management's tough on them."

Funniest Event Off the Field: One night in the late 1970s, we had a great crowd at Royals Stadium, although I don't remember the opponent. The atmosphere, as it was so often during the '70s, was electric. But the Royals were behind by four or five runs. Late in the game, the Royals started building momentum. Suddenly, Fred White and I looked down and there was a gangly fella standing on the third-base dugout, leading cheers. He almost looked as if he belonged, but remember this was long before the K-Crew. This guy was excited, dancing and waving his arms. He was fired up, possibly with a few adult beverages giving him extra courage. Two policemen came down, got to the edge of the dugout and motioned for the man to come to them, as a parent would an infant who's in trouble. The guy sheepishly walked over and they helped him down. We glanced at the action on the field and then back down at our friend.

Keep in mind, Fred and I were describing the action in the stands. It was much better. As the officers escorted the guy up the steps toward the back section on the lower level, and you figure he's headed to the slammer, he hangs his arms around the policemen's shoulders as if they're long, lost buddies. The officers were amused. They stopped at the middle walkway section and asked our fella a question. He pointed about eight rows up to an empty aisle seat. They start to walk up the stairs toward that seat. Next to the seat sits a woman who's obviously embarrassed, with her head in her hands. Obviously the wife or lady friend of our guy. The officers say something to her and she shakes her head as if to say, "Yes, that's my guy." The officers had him sit down and the gal was shaking her head that she'd keep him there. Something like that could be ugly but the police kept their cool and it turned out to be amusing. It definitely was one of our favorite moments in the stands.

Worst Transaction, Royals: It's difficult to choose just one transaction (you'll see why I'm not saying "trade") the Royals have made that really went south. In recent years, people might want to point to the deals that sent away Johnny Damon or Carlos Beltran. Former catcher Ed Hearn, who lives in Lenexa, jokes about how he was part of the worst trade — in fans' eyes, the one that sent hometown product David Cone to the New York Mets in 1987. That's a deal, frankly, that looked

OK on paper. The Royals needed a catcher and Hearn had just played in the World Series for the Mets. He just had bad luck here.

So, I'm going to go back a little further to two deals within a seven-month stretch that didn't make a lot of sense. The first was in December 1973, when the Royals traded former Rookie of the Year Lou Piniella to the Yankees for pitcher Lindy McDaniel. Throughout his career, McDaniel was a workhorse-type relief pitcher. He was a phenom, of sorts, when I was listening to the Cardinals in the 1950s because he went straight to the majors when he signed as a "bonus baby." At the time in baseball, when a player signed for a certain amount, the club had to send him directly to the majors. By the time the Royals acquired Lindy, though, he had been in the majors for 19 years. He spent two years with the Royals, going 6-5 with two saves. Lou was young and went on to a long career after leaving Kansas City.

LINDY McDANIEL: "I walked into a lion's den in Kansas City. They booed me a lot because I was traded for one of their favorite players. In my first appearance in New York after I was traded, I got a standing ovation when I came into the game. That never happened in Kansas City. I don't know if the fans were aware of what I had done previously.

"I was disappointed that I wasn't used more than I was. With the Yankees, I was under a great manager, Ralph Houk. When I came to the Royals (under Jack McKeon), it was different. I didn't pitch that often even though I was given assurance that I was wanted. I didn't feel like I fit in there like I did with the Yankees and the Cardinals. After I announced my retirement toward the end of the 1975 season, (then-manager) Whitey (Herzog) pitched me almost every game. Some of the players were astonished that I was going to retire. I just got tired of fooling around with the way I was being used."

Seven months after the Piniella-McDaniel trade, the Royals made a transaction that, I think, negatively affected the club during their play-off years, when they sold relief pitcher Gene Garber to Philadelphia in July 1974. Garber and McKeon got into a squabble about something. So, Garber was let go. Just let go. So, not only did we get rid of a great closer, but we got absolutely nothing in return. He went on to have his best years for the Phillies and the Atlanta Braves throughout the rest of the

1970s and into the '80s. Of course, we didn't have a true closer from the time Garber was let go until Dan Quisenberry got here in 1979. We had some great clubs that could've ended up in the World Series if we had a closer. Gene returned to the Royals toward the end of his career, in 1987, but his fastball wasn't as good by then.

Best Trade, Royals: Much like the "Worst Transaction," it's hard to point to just one move as being *the* best. But, much like the timing of the Piniella and Garber deals hurting the Royals, general manager Cedric Tallis made three deals with National League teams within one year exactly that built the club's strength up the middle for years to come.

The biggest of the three was on December 3, 1969, when Tallis sent Joe Foy to the Mets for pitcher Bob Johnson and a young outfielder/third baseman named Amos Otis. Bob had a great year in 1970; and, of course, A.O. went on to a star career, mainly in center-field.

Then, in June 1970, Tallis traded Fred Rico to the Cardinals for second baseman Cookie Rojas. Finally, almost a year to the day after the initial deal with the Mets, on December 2, 1970, Cedric took Johnson, who had had a good season — could throw hard and was goofier than hell — and sent him to Pittsburgh for catcher Jerry May, pitcher Bruce Dal Canton, and shortstop Fred Patek.

In those three deals, Cedric got a catcher, a pitcher, a second base-man, a shortstop and a centerfielder. Boom, the club had strength up the middle heading into its third season. I've often said and it's also been seen time and time again, if you're strong up the middle, you have a great foundation for future success.

Worst Rule: Two of them. The designated hitter and games not being suspended because of rain or snow. We covered this a couple chapters ago. But, in essence, the DH wore out its welcome during its second year of existence. And, just why are games that are stopped before the fifth inning because of the elements restarted instead of being suspend-ed?

Worst Team-Single Season: The 2003 Detroit Tigers. Coming off a 2002 campaign in which they finished 55-106, no one really expected much from the Tigers in 2003. But, this, 119 losses and only 43 wins? It's easy to say that's the worst season I've seen since 1969. That season by the Tigers is one of those times when you feel for the pitchers. Mike Maroth finished with 21 losses, Jeremy Bonderman had 19, and Nate Cornejo racked up 17. Offensively, Detroit finished last in the American League in nearly every category except triples (third with 39) and strikeouts (a whopping 1,099 as a club). On the flip side, the Tigers won 95 games just three years later.

Worst Single Play: I'd have to point to Ken Harvey getting hit in the back with a cut-off throw in, I believe, 2004. As a baseball announcer, I know by the way things are developing what's about to happen. Well, here comes a throw from the outfield with a runner trying to score. As an announcer, you anticipate the throw getting cut off. On this play, the catcher will yell to the cut-off man — while the cut-off man is watching and waiting for the throw from the outfield — whether to catch the ball or let it go. For whatever reason, maybe Harv thought he should get a visual as well as a verbal. So, he is looking at catcher John Buck and here comes the throw. You're anticipating as a broadcaster what the options are. There are many, but the ball nailing Harv in the middle of the back is not one that I had considered. But it certainly gave new meaning to the term: "Hit the cut-off man."

Worst Stadium: The Oakland Coliseum. And, believe it or not, Yankee Stadium as it continued to deteriorate over the past decade before their new park opened in 2009.

Worst Press Box/Broadcast Locations: Yankee Stadium had the worst press box. Worst location is either Oakland or Texas because you're so far from the field. The farther you are from the field, the more you feel detached from the game.

Worst Clubhouse: The worst clubhouse I ever saw was the Royals clubhouse at the old Municipal Stadium. We had the first base clubhouse, which was under the stands. The visitors' clubhouse was behind the stands on the third-base side and they had to come down a ramp in plain sight to get to the field. That was the Chiefs locker room for their games, too. I've seen pictures of them coming down that ramp.

It was old, dark and dingy. Old Tiger Stadium would be second and then Fenway Park. The main reason is that all of them are small.

Worst Playing Surface/Field: The old ballpark in Cleveland.

Worst Blow-Up By a Player: The obvious one is George Brett in the infamous "Pine Tar Game" at Yankee Stadium. Guys have thrown bats and that type of thing out of the dugout, but we've yet to see another explosion like Brett's.

Worst Blow-Up By a Manager: There have been some beauties. A lot of people would point to Hal McRae's during a post-game interview session. Lou Piniella has had some fantastic ones. Billy Martin and Earl Weaver, also, had some good ones. All of those guys have the art form of getting ejected down pretty good.

Best Interview, Royals Player: George Brett and Dan Quisenberry. I can't say enough great things about interviewing George. To this day, as pretty much anyone who's interviewed him will agree, he's a super interview. He's engaging, loves to laugh, tell stories, and is very open about whatever you ask him. In general, guys who are thoughtful and will expand, give the best interviews.

As far as Quiz, he was one of my all-time favorite Royals, not just as an interview. He was a wordsmith, always intrigued by the English language. We would give each other a word of the day, the more bizarre, the funnier. I would have to work his word into the broadcast and he would use mine in his postgame interview. His sense of humor and quotes were wonderful. As I've said often, an interview with Quiz was an adventure.

To this day, George Brett is still one of my favorite people to interview.

I've shared the story numerous times about one of my most interesting Royals interviews, but it's worth repeating. During an August game in 1969, utility infielder Juan Rios, who couldn't speak English very well, got a couple of hits and drove in a couple of runs during a Royals win. By that time in the season, the Royals were so far out of the race, and we had interviewed nearly everyone on the team, that I was running out of options. Rios was about the only player I hadn't interviewed.

On my way to Municipal Stadium the next day, I had the idea that I would interview Juan. Shoot, it might be the only real chance for him to get an interview on the pregame show since he didn't play that often. My idea was to use shortstop Jackie Hernandez, who spoke clear English, as Juan's interpreter. Jackie had helped him along all season. When I got to the park, I asked Jackie. He was up for it, as was Juan. So, the three of us, along with our producer-engineer Ed Shepherd, went down the right-field line to tape the interview. I was afraid we would get only three or four words out of Juan, and I was really sweating it.

Shep started to record and I opened with: "Our guest tonight on the Royals pregame show is Juan Rios, who drove in a couple of runs last night in the Royals' 5-2 victory. Juan doesn't speak or understand English, but Jackie Hernandez has graciously consented to be our interpreter." Then I said to Jackie, "Ask Juan his impressions and his feelings about the game last night, about his big night." I put the microphone in front of Jackie, who asked Juan the question. Juan's eyes lit up, so I put the microphone in front of Rios and he started chattering away in Spanish. I thought how this was very cool and it was working! Jackie was nodding his head and smiling. And Juan's smiling and yapping. Then they'd both laugh and keep talking. Juan was on a roll. Man, I was getting excited. We had it made. Juan stopped chatting, looked at Jackie and smiled. So I put the microphone in front of Jackie to get the interpretation. Jackie looked at me and said, "Juan said he feel pretty good."

Are you kidding me? Juan just gave us his life's story and all that came out was that he felt pretty good? To this day, I'm not sure how we stretched out that interview, but somehow we did. I guess we'll never know what great — or at least long — answer Juan gave.

Best Interview, Opponent: Frank Robinson. The reason Frank stands out is that I had heard he was a tough interview. So, I wrote down some probing questions when he was playing for Baltimore. We did the interview before a game at Municipal Stadium. We went down the foul line and I ended up doing an in-depth interview with him on hitting. One of the things I remember from that is when we were talking about players swinging at pitches on a three balls-no strike count. He said something I'll never forget: "As a big-league player to swing at a 3-0 pitch, you have to earn the right to do it."

People ask me about my "bad" or "worst" interviews, whether it's Royals players or opponents. I really haven't had many bad ones. When I started my career, Buddy Blattner knew everybody and he had done a zillion interviews, and he'd steer me toward the interesting guys. So, I never had what I would call a bad interview because I had some good info on guys who would talk and guys who wouldn't know what to say.

Best Interview, Royals Manager: Whitey Herzog. I've always enjoyed my time with managers before and after recording their pregame show. That's a time when they usually let their guard down. Whitey would *really* let his crew cut down.

Whitey startled me with his comments at times, some that we aired, others that we didn't. One night we didn't, for instance, was when he told me, "It's hard to be lucky when you're horses--t." Can life be summed up more succinctly than that?

The other one that I always liked, and always favored as a broadcaster, was when he once said, "If you're going to play horses--t, play fast." Again, another great lesson in life.

Mary Lou, Whitey's wife, told me one time that Whitey was starting to sound like Casey Stengel, who was one of his heroes. Casey had a unique way of talking sometimes. One night when the Royals hadn't been playing well, in his best Casey-ism, he said, "Yeah, we haven't been playing very well, but you're only as good as you are, and you can't do what you can't do."

Best Interview, Opposing Manager: Chuck Tanner, former Chicago White Sox.

Best Baseball Broadcaster: My dad was a Cardinal fan and from my earliest years, I remember the games being on the radio with Harry Caray, Jack Buck and Joe Garagiola. They were a tremendous team. I'd also listen to Jack Quinlan call games for the Cubs on hot summer days. Those were the most influential on my career and arguably a few of the best ever.

Best Out-of-Town Restaur-ants: Gibsons Bar and Steakhouse in Chicago is an excellent, excellent restaurant. Joseph's in Boston. I'm not even sure if that's still there. Marty Pattin knew of it from his playing days in Boston, so I went there with him. Bo Brooks in Baltimore.

Best Out-of-Town Bars: These aren't necessarily sports bars. They're local places with good atmosphere and close to where we've stayed in these cities. They're not dives. Just a good mix of people and atmosphere. Gibsons (again) in Chicago. In Boston, Daisy Buchanan's, which was owned by Derek Sanderson, who was a colorful hockey player for the Bruins. Duff's in Minnesota. The Red Onion in Texas, which was right next to the Steak & Ale there in Arlington.

Joe Garagiola had a big influence on my broadcasting career. He's one of the best ever.

The Steak & Ale was *the* place to be. In fact, at that time, it was the only place out there. Besides the Steak & Ale, the restaurant had plenty of girls and a band. I always said you could get discovered at the Steak & Ale by falling out the door — it was just one of those places where the women outnumbered the guys. It was hopping.

Fred White and I, along with most of the other Royals, were there one night after a game. Jim Wohlford, who was an outfielder for the

Fan's Question: As you watch some of the great announcers leave the game or pass on, do you ever think about your legacy?

Bryce Morris
Parkville, Missouri

Denny: I suppose it's safe to say that I hope people thought the game was described accurately and what I described was vivid in their mind's eye in telling both sides of the story. I always try to entertain. There are so many elements to a baseball broadcast. Obviously what's happening on the field, but you have other games to talk about, players' backgrounds, and you try to throw in some humor and have some fun. We try to keep it light. And, since fans are so different and want so many different things, I hope we've given them what they've wanted through the years.

Royals, came up to the bar where Fred and I were talking. Wolfy squeezed in between us. He had been having problems offensively, and he wasn't saying much, and he wasn't too involved in the conversation. When things got a little bit quiet, he looked at Fred and me and said, "Guys, will you pray with me?"

Understandably, the request threw most of us off base. Praying is a good thing, but we were in a bar with loud music and a lot of commotion. Fred looked at him and said, "Well, Wolfy, I'm not sure this is the time or the place."

Wolfy replied, "I really, really have to get rid of this slump. Won't you please pray with me?"

Fred thought for a second before saying, "How about if I just buy you a beer?"

* * *

When you're around this game for any amount of time, you see some incredible moments and some maddening things from the best of the best. And, just when you think you've seen it all, something remarkable or goofy happens. That's what keeps us coming back, game after game, year after year. And it's the reason I love this game of baseball.

INDEX

ABOUT THE AUTHORS

Denny Matthews has been with the Kansas City Royals as a radio announcer since the club's first season, 1969. He teamed with Buddy Blattner until 1975, and then became the team's number-one announcer, working for 25 years with Fred White, who joined the Royals in 1973. Besides working for the Royals, Matthews has worked games for the CBS Radio Network. He is one of a few broadcasters in baseball that has broadcast exclusively for the same team, without interruption, in five different decades. After the 2003 season, the Royals selected Matthews for the club's Hall of Fame. Then, in 2007, Matthews received the Ford C. Frick Award, the highest honor for an announcer from the National Baseball Hall of Fame. Matthews, a 1966 graduate of Illinois Wesleyan, lettered in baseball and football for three years, and finished eighth in the nation in the NAIA for pass receiving in 1965. Matthews has co-authored the books *Play by Play: 25 Years of Royals on Radio* and *Tales from the Royals Dugout.*

Matthews is an avid golfer and hockey player. He resides in the Kansas City area.

Matt Fulks, who started his journalism career while attending Lipscomb University in Nashville, Tennessee, after his baseball career was cut short by a lack of ability, spends his time as a free-lance writer, editor and co-host of a syndicated radio show, "Behind the Stats." He is a regular contributor to various publications, including kcmetrosports.com — the Web site for Kansas City's all-sports TV station Metro Sports — and the Royals' *Gameday* magazine. He is the author/co-author of 13 other books, including *Echoes of Kansas Basketball, More Than the Score*, and *Good As Gold*, co-authored with Frank White. More information is available at www.mattfulks.com. Matt resides in the Kansas City area with his wife Libby and their three children.